This is the story of the men and women who answer the nation's 911 calls for help, who man the radios for law enforcement officers, firefighters, and emergency services personnel. The nameless voices that calm terrified victims and help emergency resources to the scene are rarely given credit.

How are Public Safety Telecommunicators selected? Who trains them and are there mandatory job training standards? When did the radio first come into use? How did 911 get its start? What is TERT or a TAC?

Come along for a journey behind the scenes to world where one shift is never the same as the previous. Shifts are moments of controlled chaos broken up by periods of tedium. Welcome to the nation's Communications Centers and the world of Public Safety Dispatchers.

What is Your Emergency? The History of Public Safety Dispatching in America

"What is Your Emergency?"

The History of Public Safety Dispatching in America

second edition

By Diana Sprain

What is Your Emergency? The History of Public Safety Dispatching in America

Copyright 2016 Diana Sprain

All rights reserved. No part of this publication may be reproduced, stored in a retrieval system, or transmitted in any form or by any means, electronic, mechanical, recording or otherwise, without prior written permission of the author except for brief quotations for reviews of the work.

Table of Contents

Acknowledgments...6
Foreword..8
Introduction...11
Chapter One: Foundations of Public Safety....................15
Chapter Two: Attention All Units- Public Safety Embraces the Radio..30
Chapter Three: Civilians Take Over................................44
Chapter Four: Public Safety Gets Organized...................57
Chapter Five: 9-1-1: I Know Where You Are....................73
Chapter Six: Public Safety Dispatching as a Profession...88
Chapter Seven: How the Public Perceives Us..................102
Chapter Eight: 911 on Television....................................112
Chapter Nine: Dispatcher Standards: Building the bar but where are the Standards?..117
Chapter Ten: Updating the System...............................125
Chapter Eleven: Major Incidents and Disasters.............133
Chapter Twelve: Doing the Job......................................151
Chapter Thirteen: The Survey..171
Helpful Websites..191
Bibliography..193
Author Biography

What is Your Emergency? The History of Public Safety Dispatching in America

Acknowledgments

This book has been a dream of mine for many years. Even with my lifetime of dispatching experience, I still couldn't have completed this work without assistance from many people. If I have left any of you out, I apologize, it was not intentional. First, I must thank my husband, Sam, for putting up with my countless hours of bending over the keyboard of my laptop instead of paying attention to you. I love you honey – you're the best!

To my co-workers, David, Grace, Kayla, Susan, and Kasen who inadvertently gave me ideas or suffered through my silence as I worked on chapters during the 'quiet' times – thanks, guys! To Sergeant Michael Holland (ret.) of the Berkeley (CA) Police Department: thank you for the information on August Vollmer. A universal-sized thanks and Rest in Peace to my late co-worker and friend, Gary Allen who passed away in 2015. His website, "911Dispatch" is archieved on the web and has a plethora of information and audio tapes for training. Thanks to Randall Larson for a copy of his article on the history of 9-1-1 Magazine along with some nice encouraging words in his response to my inquiry. Check out 9-1-1 Magazine on-line for articles and photographs about public safety and dispatch. A thousand thanks go out to Sue Pivetta of Professional Pride, for the inspirational words and suggestions to improve the book as a whole. She gave me permission to use whatever I wanted from her website 911Trainer.com.

My eternal thanks for the detailed information on the origins of APCO's founding from Rick Rybicki, the APCO Historical Chairperson. For information about old radios and communications equipment from the Emergency Medical Services Virtual Museum, thanks go to Fred 'Mother' Swihart, the Curator of the EMS Museum. For permission to use their survey results of training and the challenges of today, my thanks goes out to Caitlin Kingsley, Marketing Director of PowerPhone. A shout-out for some wonderful photographs of MetComm's IDT team sent by Paul

Smith, Executive Director of Metropolitan Area Communications Center (MetComm). I'm sorry I couldn't use the picture in this book. I'm hoping future updates will allow me to do so. A heartfelt thanks to Mr. Arnold Shapiro, producer extraordinaire of 'Rescue 911' for an exclusive interview. You are our (dispatchers) hero for showing the public what we did! To every dispatcher who filled out and sent back my survey, BLESS you!! And, finally, to the countless dispatchers who through comments on my blog, Facebook page, or Twitter, added their two cents to help me along. Even a single sentence of encouragement made a difference.

    This second edition of my book corrects a few minor errors and adds some more information. Thank you for reading my book!

What is Your Emergency? The History of Public Safety Dispatching in America

Foreword

Why would I write a book about Public Safety Dispatchers? Who would read it and why would anyone care?

In High School I had no idea what a dispatcher was nor did I care. My career goal was to become a paramedic. I had fallen in love with the television show *Emergency!* and wanted to help people, just like Johnny and Roy. Taking the mandatory career tests, paramedic wasn't even a choice (for that matter, neither was dispatcher). After certifying as an Emergency Medical Technician in 1978, I couldn't wait to get a job with an ambulance company and start running calls.

EMT pay was lousy way back then (pennies over minimum wage). I was offered the chance to learn dispatching to cover for breaks and vacations. I had no life at 18, so any opportunity to get overtime was welcome. Just like Raquel Welch in *Mother, Juggs & Speed*, I didn't really want to be in dispatch, I wanted to be out in the field taking care of patients. It was a profession heavily dominated by men and it came with a lot of hazing (the complainers & whiners didn't last). The few women in the field were tough and assertive. No one pushed us around without getting a healthy dose back.

I had been the first female EMT hired by a compnay called McNulty EMS and when it went belly up I had to find another job. While waiting for an EMT slot, I took a full-time dispatcher position with another company in a not-so nice area. The company was in the process of upgrading to a computer-aided dispatch system but also required us to log radio traffic on paper logs. What a pain.

Mt family pressured me to take a different dispatching job for one of the few ambulance companies still based out of a mortuary service closer to home (okay, let the jokes begin), again waiting for an EMT slot to open up. When calls stacked (more calls than available units to handle them), administrative personnel would step in to the cimmunications center and my dispatch partner & I (we were both EMTs) would use a spare rig and run calls. No big deal, right? Keep in mind, dispatchers handled front counter duties.

by Diana Sprain

Because of this, we had to adhere to strict dress code standards (men wore jackets and slacks, women dresses or skirts). That's how we ran calls, too. Sure, and didn't we turn a few heads at the emergency rooms?

I discovered I had a knack for dispatching. I tried to find out more about the job but kept coming up with dead ends. Most of the books on law enforcement, fire fighting, or emergency medical services referred to radios in the barest terms. And dispatchers? Well, we were treated as necessary evils. I believe the feeling was (and still is) due to a misunderstanding. Field personnel don't know the true scope of our job.

In 1982, I was working for Allied Ambulance as an EMT. Allied contracted to the City of Oakland (CA) to provide emergency medical services from the east end of the city(starting at Lake Merritt to the San Leandro border (including Alameda and Bay Farm Islands). In August of that year, the County was initiating their paramedic program but the majority of the runs were handled by basic life support (BLS) crews. Allied's dispatchers would take calls from the County Sheriff. I worked nights, running an average of 12-14 calls in twelve hours. I loved it. The fun didn't last for me because I found myself pregnant. Allied's management wasn't sure what to do with me. They'd never had a crew member need time from the field for maternity leave before. How long could I run calls? It was decided to let me stay in the field until I started 'showing'.

Once I had to stop working in the ambulance, I was offered the chance to take a relief dispatch position: two nights, two swings, and one day. I never knew what time of day it was but the position led to a full-time job as a Public Safety Dispatcher with the City of Berkeley (CA).

My life's true calling had just begun.

When my family and friends asked what I was doing, I had to explain what the job was. Most didn't understand. They thought I was an operator, just like the phone company. Really, how hard was it to answer a phone call? Many had never had to call for the police, fire, or an ambulance. The few that had wanted to tell me how great (or bad) the service was. Could I do something about

What is Your Emergency? The History of Public Safety Dispatching in America

their experience? Why did it take sooooo long? Why did 'x' or 'y' happen? Why did the dispatcher ask so many 'stupid' questions?

Why indeed?

I was fortunate in my ems dispatching and field experience. It helped me to get a position as a Public Safety Dispatcher. It helped but the two were night and day different. Working at a Public Safety Answering Point (PSAP), or 911 Center, was a new world.

I like to think my experience on both sides of the radio have given me the perspective to write this book. As a tail-end Baby Boomer, the technological changes I've witnessed are incredible. I can remember a time before personal answering machines, cell phones, computers, 24 hour television, cable television, and computer games. I remember when 911 was phone number only – if your city even had 911.

This book is an attempt to answer the questions of my family, friends, and those I've heard on interviews on too many news broadcasts, seen in magazine articles, or just heard in passing. Dispatchers are part of the Public Safety system –we are the hidden voice, the unsung 'first' first responders. We've been ignored for too long. No more are we to be a small paragraph or footnote in a textbook. On behalf of the men and women behind the radio and answering the phones in dispatch centers across the USA, welcome to our world. It's a crazy ride.

It is time our story is told.

by Diana Sprain

Introduction: Dispatching is a highly specialized and rigorous endeavor in its own right

"My baby isn't breathing!"
"Our house is on fire! What should we do?"
"7B14 shots fired, shots fired! Jones and Oakdale…"
"Hi, my car is missing. I think it's been stolen."
"2219, code 3 medical, 1876 Marshal Road."
"Hello, my friend cut his leg and it's bleeding real bad."
"There's been a boat accident."
"We're lost in a snowstorm, please can you help us?"
"Control, 1L15 stopping one at 5th and Maple."

What do all of the above statements have in common? At first glance, it is easy enough to see that some of the statements are a cry for help while others are radio transmissions between field units and the base station. One can tell the above statements are a mixture of fire, law enforcement and medical responses, so what links all of those calls together? What are the common grounds between the frightened callers and the field personnel? The Public Safety Telecommunicator is the common thread, the link that connects the chain.

Dr. Jeff Clawson said in his book, *Principles of Emergency Medical Dispatch*, "…Dispatching is a highly specialized and rigorous endeavor in its own right. It is time that that the respect owing this group be shown -and demanded - by the dispatchers themselves!"

The Public Safety Telecommunicator, henceforth referred to as a dispatcher, is the one person who is involved in every incident, whether or not emergency field units are dispatched. Even when an event is witnessed and called in over the radio or telephone, a dispatcher is still involved. In some cases, a situation may be resolved without the need to send a firefighter, paramedic, or law enforcement officer. Dispatchers are that vital part in the Public Safety pyramid, of which the system could not exist today without them.

What is Your Emergency? The History of Public Safety Dispatching in America

The job title varies: Public Safety Telecommunicator, Public Safety Dispatcher, Emergency Medical Dispatcher, Call-Taker, Emergency Operator, or Emergency Communicators Dispatcher but the job is basically the same. Dispatchers collect information from a source (or multiple sources), decide on a course of action, and then dispatch the appropriate field personnel to handle the situation. On occasion, the call for service may be out-sourced to non-emergency division (animal control or public works) or transferred to another agency which has the jurisdictional authority for the response.

In simplest terms, the Dispatcher takes a phone call, obtains the facts, and dispatches the police, fire units, or an ambulance.

So, why does the communications profession have few members actually make it to retirement age compared to the amount actually performing the job? Why is it difficult to get a position as a dispatcher in the first place? Why does the profession have a high turnover rate as compared to law enforcement officers or firefighters? How long has dispatching as a job been around? What is required of the dispatchers now verses when the profession first came into existence? Has the media helped or hindered the job performance of dispatchers? How do other Public Safety personnel view dispatchers?

The scenario to obtain assistance is known to most of the residents of this great country of ours. Whether the call for help is for a family member having a heart attack, a structure fire, a traffic accident or a crime, the best way to get assistance is to dial 9-1-1. We all expect the phone to be answered within a few seconds by a live person who is supposed to know where we're at without being told. The professional Public Safety Dispatcher asks a couple of quick questions and we get the assistance within a short amount of time.

Calls to 9-1-1 follow that basic process most of the time, although not always without incident. With cell phones and Voice over Internet Phone (VoIP), locations aren't always apparent. People traveling with cell phones enter local police numbers and hit auto dial, not thinking about the issues of who responds when they call for help when they are out of state – or even out of the

by Diana Sprain

country. With funding and staff cuts in other departments, Mr. & Mrs. John Q. Citizen inundate Public Safety Answering Points (PSAPs – also known as Communications Centers) with calls for service, including questions on major incidents, non-emergency information requests, weather & road status inquiries, and even going as far as to ask what time it is.

Is it fair to blame the dispatcher when a call for service doesn't go smoothly? The media, and public, are quick to point fingers when a problem occurs. The communications center staff responds with accusations of their own, claiming they are understaffed and over-burdened with mandatory overtime. Where are the media when the millions of calls go off without a hitch?

The National Emergency Number Association (NENA) estimates over 240 million calls are made to 9-1-1 PSAPs every year; add in the non-emergency calls to the listed seven-digit numbers and the 3-1-1 system (set up for non-emergency service, but not available in all areas), and one can deduce that our nation's Public Safety Telecommunicators are busy people. In small to medium size agencies, the dispatchers handle both phone calls and radio traffic compared to large departments where law enforcement may have a separate center from the fire & emergency medical services (in some cases, fire and ems may be individual centers as well). With the change from hand-written (manual) records to a computer-aided dispatch (CAD) system, more agencies are faced with a higher turnover rate. Not only are our nation's PSAPs having trouble retaining dispatchers; those who stay are asked to do more with less staffing. In some cases, they have taken a pay cut to keep their jobs!

The Federal Communications Commission (FCC) chairman called for a nationwide Public Safety radio network, with regional consolidated communications centers instead of local 911 PSAPs. With budget concerns a major issue, will Genachowski's dream come to fruition? It is difficult to say. There already been agencies on both sides of the fence in regards to consolidation: dispatchers having lost jobs when the move was approved and others keeping their jobs in at least one case when a city voted to keep their dispatch center.

What is Your Emergency? The History of Public Safety Dispatching in America

This book is the story of those men and women: the true Public Safety First Responders.

by Diana Sprain

Chapter One: Foundations of Public Safety

The ancients knew best

The roots of modern Public Safety are found deep in history. Draco, a Greek nobleman was passionate in his belief of a lawful society. He presented his code of laws to his fellow noblemen in 621 BCE. Draco's rules were heavily biased towards the upper echelon, instead of being fair to all members of society. The Greek lawmaker also was rather harsh in setting penalties: many property crime violations carried a death penalty. To this day, a 'draconian measure' refers back to this man.

The Romans based their version of a civil society using the Twelve Tables on the people they conquered. The Tables included a process for court in civil cases. For example, if a plaintiff was unable to get to court on his own feet, he was required to be brought by a litter. Claiming illness was no excuse according to Roman law. The Twelve Tables stayed in effect until around the early sixth century, when the Justinian legislation took precedence.

The Romans had a law enforcement of the government called the Quaestores Paricidii. These specially trained men tracked down those accused of homicide. Quaestores worked in pairs, bringing the captured criminal back to Rome to stand before the Praetor. A trial would be held before the public, with Roman legionnaires armed with wooden staves (instead of their usual swords) present to control the crowd if needed.

Romans turned an eye towards other safety issues as well. Marcus Licinius Crassus started a fire watch with men ready to respond to reported fires. Marcus didn't have his men show up out of the goodness of his heart. The property owner was expected to pay for the fire suppression. If the owner refused to negotiate, Marcus had his men stand back and they watched the structure burn. Another Roman, Caesar Augustus, formed his own fire service called the Vigiles Urbani, with his men using buckets, pumps, and other commonly firefighting equipment. Caesar was creative with his funding for the watch, adding a tax to the sale of slaves. Augustus' fire department had up to one thousand men,

What is Your Emergency? The History of Public Safety Dispatching in America

grouped in divisions called *cohorts*. The cohorts also did a little policing when the rabble caused problems. Both men weren't above buying out burnt property afterwards, for a hefty profit. After the Roman Empire crumbled, the people under the Eagle's shadow broke in to smaller kingdoms and warrior societies.

The Saxons and Danes swore an oath to the crown called a Frankpledge when they turned 12 years of age. A leader, or *Chief*, was designated for every ten men, and that leader was responsible for the conduct of those men. Ten bands of pledges, or one hundred men, were a *tithing*. The land was broke up in parts referred to as a *hundred* for administrative purposes. A hundred was equal to a piece of land able to sustain one hundred people and had a *Chief Pledge*. Shires were divided to *tithings* as well. A portion of land that could only support one family was called a '*hide*'. The *Shire* was in charge of the hundred, and the person who held the seat of the Shire was the *Reeve*.

Just after William the Conqueror won his throne at Hastings, he designated the *Reeve* to dispense justice and collect taxes in the shires. The name of the person handing these duties eventually became known as a 'Sheriff'. The good 'ol Sheriff went around with his faithful *Bailiff* to help him in case of trouble. A duty for all residents was an immediate response to any *Hue and Cry*. Medieval law required all able-bodied persons to help search for the wanted subject once the Hue and Cry was announced.

In the twelfth century legal reforms were instituted by King Henry II. He continued the Old Saxon style of courts and initiated travelling justices. The King's exchequer heard cases involving royal monies & taxes at Caen and at Westminster for Royal civil matters. Henry allowed the *trials by combat* and *trials by ordeal* throughout his reign. New laws were called *Writs*. Copies of writs had a large King's Seal attached (the Seal had a picture of the King on his throne on one side and mounted on his horse ready to defend the Kingdom on the other) by a ribbon. Anyone could buy a personal copy of a writ for a small fee.

Considered a bad King, John the youngest son of King Henry II inherited an almost bankrupt kingdom after the death of King Richard the Lionhearted. On top of an empty treasury, John turned aside decent advisors and kept his 'yes-men' at his side. The mistakes, paired with his lack of training for the job of king, resulted in the loss of territories on the mainland and more abuses towards his barons. Fed-up, the nobility rebelled - the result being the Magna Carta, the document which became one of the foundations of the Articles of Confederation. The Magna Carta was also the inspiration for the Declaration of Independence and the U.S. Constitution. This legislation officially gave the circuit judges power over local authorities and the sheriff.

In 1254, French King Saint Louis passed a resolution allowing citizens to have night-watches of their own, in addition to the King's men. By 1284, England's King Edward I enacted the Statute of Winchester, which established Constables and Chief Constables to take over the outdated Frank Pledge system. Constables also were allowed to keep weapons in their homes, set up fire watches & rotate the duty, do their best to prevent crime, and even ensure the street lamps were lit at night.

Another important step was the Justice of the Peace Act of 1361. This allowed the official to take the accused in custody, do the initial investigation, and submit the findings to the higher courts. Only by conferring with another justice, could a person be allowed to pay bail. This prevented a subject from bribing the court official. Justice appointments were influenced by local population while Sheriffs were selected by the Monarch.

On December 29, 1386 a large crowd gathered at a French monastery in Paris to watch two men fight to the death. It was the last sanctioned duel in medieval Europe. Sir Jean de Carrouges returned from his duty in Scotland to find his wife Marguerite assaulted. The rape resulted in a pregnancy. Sir Jean's wife accused Squire Jacques Le Gris of committing the crime. The case went through the local courts and all the way to King Charles. The country became divided: was Le Gris guilty or did de Carrouges have a vendetta for his former friend? After hours of hacking at one another on horseback, Le Gris impaled de Carrouges' horse with his lance (there were no rules for this type of fight). In return, Carrouges took out his enemy's horse. The men continued fighting on foot both taking wounds. In the end, Sir Jean killed Le Gris, proclaiming God was on his side. As with many major legal battles, there were allegations of wrongdoing by both parties and they did have a history together. Did Marguerite have an affair or did her husband desire Le Gris' holdings? Only the two men truly knew the answers.

Help, help, my home is burning.

The colonists settling in the Americas were cognizant of fire danger. The city of New York had banned wooden chimneys in 1648, also placing an order for leather buckets, ladders, and hooks to aid in fighting any future fires. A call went out for volunteers to participate in night watch duties. Boston established their fire department in 1678, complete with an imported hand pump from the mother country, England. Benjamin Franklin is often credited with creating the concept of the fire department in the United States, but manual fire pumps had been in use by departments in Germany since the 1500's. The Great Fire of London in 1666 resulted in insurance companies starting a pay for protection service. The fire departments were supplying bronze markers to their clients to place above the door. When a fire was reported, the responders looked for the markers. Of course, one's neighbors might help in suppressing a fire of structures not under the protection of the fire companies. After all, fire was a danger to all.

Benjamin Franklin didn't invent the concept of the fire service he just took an idea in use and improved upon it. He supplied markers to subscribers. The unfortunate resident or business owner who didn't have the metal symbol of the fire protection on his entry above the door had to fight his own fire. Yes, the fire department responded, but only to protect structures of their members.

Jan Van der Heyden designed a working fire hose in 1672, made of leather with couplings every fifteen feet to work in conjunction with hand pumps. Before the fire hose, the pumps couldn't generate enough pressure to be efficient. Another breakthrough came in 1725, when Richard Newsham redesigned the fire engine. With Newsham's improvements, teams of men working the pump were able to shoot a stream of water 120 feet in to the air at 160 gallons a minute. In Boston and other major cities, leaders were pushing for stricter builder codes. Many prominent citizens were members of the fire brigades, included George Washington.

England started manufacturing rubber fire hoses in about 1820. In 1853 Cincinnati, Ohio began the first fully paid fire department. They were one of the first to use steam-driven fire apparatus, as well. Horse-drawn fire apparatus were brought in to use in the early nineteenth century. Firefighters took great pride in their fire horses. The brave animals quickly learned their job, running to their place when the alarm bell went off. Many a retired fire horse was seen to follow the fire engines to fires if given the opportunity.

In mid-1800's, Moses Farmer and William F. Channing developed a fire alarm box by modifying telegraph technology. The fire services came to rely on fire alarm boxes. The devices began popping up in key areas, along with fire hydrants. See a fire, pull the alarm box. It was simple and easy to find and activate. Once the alarm was pulled an alarm would sound at a central monitoring point. The person watching the panel of alarms would notify the appropriate fire stations.

Telegraphs and electricity led to new inventions. A machine called a typeprinting telegraph was designed by David Edward Hughs, with simultaneous work by Siemens & Creed. This device was adopted by the telephone companies and supplied to police departments. Alexander Graham Bell made the first working telephone device. Bell and his assistant, Thomas A. Watson, performed the first successful test on March 10, 1876. The Library of Congress has Alexander's journal, of which one can view his notes and diagrams. History has a skewed memory of the days' event. Alexander did not say, "Watson, come here I need you." According to his notes, he carefully recorded his words spoken over his device as, "Mr. Watson – come here – I want to see you." Alexander never spilled any acid of any sort on himself.

What is Your Emergency? The History of Public Safety Dispatching in America

His Majesty's top cops show the way.

Henry and John Fielding established the first paid law enforcement agency in London during the mid eighteenth century. Henry was an advocate for the law enforcement profession, having self published pamphlets, encouraging the government to curtail the increasing crime rate. One such paper focused on robberies, was entitled, *Inquiry into the Causes of the Late Increase of Robbers* and was published in 1751. The brothers called their agency the *Thames River Runners.* John and Henry had a radical idea about law enforcement for their day: instead of dealing with the aftermath of a crime, why not patrol and to *prevent* the incident in the first place? Prior to the Fielding Brothers, no one had truly considered a proactive response to law enforcement. After the brothers died, a mounted unit was established, called the *Bow Street River Patrol* in 1805, even receiving some funding from the government.

Horse back patrols were first used in 1673 for a short amount of time. In 1800, the mounted unit was re-established again. This time the horse patrol members wore uniforms, earning the nickname of 'Robin RedBreasts'.

Another unique style of law enforcement was a marine patrol service. Patrick Colquhoun liked what the Fielding Brothers had done and believed the water ways should be as safe as the roads and cities. England depended heavily on its rivers and locks to transport goods. The Thames was a major transportation channel to the coast. Using privately donated funds, he created the Thames River Police Department: the first full-time, paid police department.

Sir Robert Peel, the man many law enforcement historians consider the founder of the modern police department, started his career in Ireland as the Chief Secretary in Ireland in 1812, established the Royal Irish Constabulary in 1814. Along with the usual crimes, Sir Robert had to contend with the IRA terrorist bombing attacks.

The English government offered Sir Peel the office of the Home Secretary in 1822. As Home Secretary, he was in charge of domestic affairs. An enthusiastic advocate of law enforcement, Sir Robert introduced a bill to Parliament which would begin create the Metropolitan Police District at Scotland Yard. The bill passed on July 19, 1829. The small private companies, which included the Bow Street foot patrol, the Robin RedBreast mounted units, and the Thames River Police, were all integrated in to England's Metropolitan Police.

Sir Peel selected two men to head up the new Metropolitan Police: Charles Rowan, a retired Army Colonel, and Richard Mayne, a lawyer. The two men divided the force in to seventeen districts. They made the Metropolitan force a paramilitary organization. Many of the initial policies & procedures were adopted by later departments. Peel's baby was the model for law enforcement agencies across the world. Sir Robert was so highly thought of he was elected Prime Minister of England twice, the first time from 1834 to 1835 and the second time 1841 through 1846 but he allegedly didn't have a good working relationship with Queen Victoria.

The early 1900's were exciting years for science. Hans Christian Oersted developed his electrical communicating device. Next, in England, William Sturgeon invented the electromagnet in 1825. In 1837, two scientists, also Englishmen, William Cooke and Charles Wheatstone invented a working telegraph. Over in North America, Samuel Morse was working on his own devices. Morse came up with his own telegraph design and his data transmission system (Morse code) revolutionized telecommunications. The Transcontinental Telegraph test was done in 1844 and the line set up for actual use in 1861.

The New York Police Department made the change from a constable system to a uniformed police department after a bill was passed in 1845, urged on by Mayor William Havemayer. Mayor Havemayer appointed George Matsell as the first Chief of Police. Life as a New York City Police Officer was very different in the 19th century. Politics played a large role in the duties of a patrolman, as did gambling and vice. Officers were called on to supervise elections and allegiance was bought with the promise of a job.

What is Your Emergency? The History of Public Safety Dispatching in America

In 1895, Theodore Roosevelt was appointed President of the New York City Police Commission. Prior to his appointment as President of the NYC Commission, Roosevelt had served on a Special Commission to investigate the local government of the City and County of New York. One of the recommendations was to change the way police officers were hired by the New York City Police from a private system to a civil service system. The hope was to cut down on the corruption and special favors the appointment system had long endorsed. (Foster 646-675)

Teddy did his best to reform the New York City PD. He set down disciplinary rules, established a bicycle unit, and made annual physical exams mandatory. No longer were officers hired because of their political connections. Any man could apply for a job, and providing he met the job requirements, become a law enforcement officer.

The Innovators

A survey of the electrical industry, as part of the 1902 census, noted that "there were 148 electrical police-patrol systems. Of these, 125 were exclusively telephone, and three were a combination of the two. The first call-boxes utilized the telegraph in a one-way system to the station. An electrical signal mechanism was placed along the route of the patrolman and connected by circuit wires to the headquarters or precinct station. Some of these call boxes were placed against a convenient wall or on a lamp post, but early practice favored specialty constructed booth on curbs or street corners."

Patrolmen would do periodic check-ins to the local police station by inserting their keys. A signal was sent to the station, registering the time and location of the callbox on a recording tape. Requests for assistance, wagons, ambulances, and other types of calls could be sent depending on a series of codes. The system worked, but there was room for improvement.

An innovator was turning heads on the west coast. In the city of Berkeley (CA), in 1905, August Vollmer was elected Town Marshall. The young man started his career in public service as a mailman. If delivering the U.S. mail wasn't enough, he signed up to become a volunteer firefighter. Vollmer started his law enforcement career in Berkeley by increasing the department from three men to twelve, allowing for day and night patrol. Vollmer was big on scientific methods in policing. Vollmer believed police officers should be taught the fundamentals of police science and in 1908 brought university staff and police officers together to iron out his idea for a formal academy.

The job title was changed from Marshal to Police Chief in 1909. In 1916, Vollmer talked a local professor, Dr. Albert Schneider, into becoming the first Criminalist, using his knowledge in pharmacology & bacteriology to solve crimes. The Chief added bicycle patrolmen to prove that officers could respond quicker on bikes than on foot. August put his men in vehicles in 1917. Under August's urging police officer John Larson developed the polygraph machine. August also served a brief stint as chief of the Los Angeles Police Department, before returning back to Berkeley Police. Later Vollmer was appointed the Chairman of the Wickersham Commission by President Herbert Hoover in 1929, which studied the effects of Prohibition on law enforcement.

August quickly calculated the value of the call box system, albeit a modified version. Why not? The devices had worked for the fire service. Call boxes were installed for the beat cops. Reporting parties came to the station or called in to the desk officer. The facts were gathered by the desk officer. The next step was to get the call information out to the beat officers. No problem, flip a switch and a light went on near the call box for that beat (or district's) officer. As soon as he (and let's face reality, back then the officers were primarily men), the patrolman would walk to the box and insert his key, call the station and soon enough be on his way to meet with the distraught citizen.

In Los Angeles, Charles Foster, a private detective, came up with an idea for a recall system. As part of the services his company, Foster Private Patrol Services, offered, Charles would 'patrol' his area on a bicycle, watching for suspicious subjects, prowlers, or burglars. Mr. Foster had made arrangements with Home Telephone Company to rig red lights on nine telephone

What is Your Emergency? The History of Public Safety Dispatching in America

poles throughout the area he covered. The red lights were connected to his residence, where the panel was watched by his wife. Mr. Foster directed the companies he worked for contact his wife if they had any problems or concerns about their properties they wanted him to check out. In turn, Mrs. Foster would switch on the red lights in the intersections. Charles Foster, riding on his bicycle, would see the red lights as he checked the properties contracted to his company and know to call home. It might be said that Charles was one of the first canine officers, since he was known to travel with his fox terrier. The dog, Mac, would help Foster locate the suspects once he arrived at the scene.

Law enforcement agencies took note of Foster's success, soon installing lights in their jurisdictions. Recall lights could be flashed in a series of codes, similar to the Morse code system. August read about Charles Foster's system in a newspaper article. August and Foster were soon corresponding back and forth. It didn't take long for Berkeley Police's August Vollmer to take a trip to Los Angeles to check out the red light system for himself. Soon, BPD had its own red lights suspended from selected intersections, with the assistance of Gamewell Signal and Alarm Company.

A few cities went further, installing red lights on top of buildings. When the desk officer wanted a particular beat officer to call the station, he would flip a switch, which lit up a light corresponding to the beat. The field unit would call in via the call box, and obtain the call assignment.

The boxes in Berkeley allowed for lights or bells. The bells had limited audible range, but lights mounted higher up were easier to see by the field personnel. Berkeley Police boxes had seven types of codes for beat cops to transmit to the station. Status checks were still answered as 'rings' on the radio long after the call boxes and lights went out of use in Berkeley for years by veteran officers and dispatchers. The radio dispatcher using a status check code would call an officer's badge number, who would reply by answering 'ring' over the radio channel. The old ways have changed, the Berkeley Police long since switched to beat identifiers from using officer's badge numbers. Even today, some cities still have remnants of the old fashioned lights still on tops of some buildings. With all the innovations August Vollmer set in place he couldn't have done it alone. The Berkeley Police Chief needed cooperation from the criminal justice system. Alameda County District Attorney Earl Warren served the citizens from 1920 to 1924 and again from 1925 to 1938. He and his staff backed Chief Vollmer and his new ideas. Warren eventually was elected Attorney General and later Governor of Detroit (MI)

Police had joined the technological age in the 1920's. Detroit Police Commissioner William P. Rutledge wanted to have have top of the line equipment. He knew that to solve crime, you had to get the information out to the beat cops fast, and that meant better communications directly with field personnel.

Encouraging his men to experiment, three radio cars went on patrol on April 7, 1922. The radio could only transmit from dispatch to the vehicles but it beat the telegraph process that other law enforcement agencies had instituted. Information didn't have to wait for a patrolman to see a red, get to a callbox, and call the station. Rutledge's radio cars were a success.

Orlando W. Wilson was involved with law enforcement for most of his life. He started as a policeman for the City of Berkeley when August Vollmer was Chief of Police. After getting an education at UC Berkeley Orlando moved to Southern California, where he was named Chief of Police at Fullerton (CA). His next stop was Wichita Police. During his time at Wichita Police Department, he conquered corruption, increased standards for officer hires (college educations), and going along with his experience at Berkeley, introduced patrol vehicles with radios and a crime lab. Orlando, or O.W., later was appointed Superintendent of the Chicago Police Department by Mayor Richard Daley.

San Francisco was the site for the International Association of Fire Engineers Conference in 1922. During the gathering, the attendees were given an opportunity to see how the new mobile radio system worked by RCA technicians. A base station set-up was installed within the San Francisco Civic Auditorium. An operator broadcast signals, which were picked up by fire units driving around in the City. The test impressed the attendees, leaving radio companies smiling. The age of telecommunications was alive and well.

"Je le pansai, dieu le guerit."

The above phase translates as "I bandaged him, and God healed him." was attributed to 16th century French surgeon Ambroise Pare. He was supposed to have said this about his battlefield surgery techniques, although one could consider the real *first medics* to be the Knights Hospitallers, who took care of the injured and sick during the Crusades. The Hospitallers established hospitals in the Holy Lands to care for those who needed extended care. Another Frenchman, Dominique Jean Larrey came up with a way of sorting through the casualties, calling his technique *triage*. To triage patients, one takes the most severely wounded patients that have the best chances for surviving their wounds away first while letting those who will take up the most resources (with little or no chance of recovering) alone. Triage may seem harsh but in a mass casualty incident, there is no other choice with limited personnel & resources.

Larrey removed the patients from the battlefield by horse-drawn ambulances, transporting them away to a safe location for treatment. The Spanish used ambulances to remove the wounded in 1487. Treating wounded men at the scene of a battle wasn't new, for any person could slap on a dressing. It was the French, during the Napoleonic Wars who are credited with advancing medical treatments for wounded soldiers.

For many decades Emergency Medical Services (EMS) was handled on a 'you call, we haul' style, using 'Cadillac' ambulances run by funeral parlors, volunteers, based out of hospital ER's, or rescue units manned by police officers out of police stations. Most of the cost was covered by patient pay, volunteer fund-raising or donations. Ambulance attendants received minimal training, if at all, via the Red Cross or during time served in the military. There was little standard of care; advanced services were provided when a physician or RN accompanied the crew.

by Diana Sprain

Modern Emergency Medical Services originated in Europe. According to James Page in his book, *The Paramedics,* "In Russia, for example, the concept of out-of-hospital patient care may have begun as early as 1918. It is believed that the Russians began dispatching ambulance crews consisting of a doctor, a nurse, and a special physician's assistant sometime prior to 1960. Dr. Rudolph Frey, in Mainz, Germany, began placing doctors in ambulance vehicles as early as 1961. At about the same time, doctors began serving in pre-hospital care roles in Toulouse, France, also...The foreigner who was to have the greatest influence on Emergency Medical Services in America, however, was J. Frank Pantridge, physician in charge of the Department of Cardiology at Belfast's Royal Victoria Hospital and Professor of Cardiology at that city's Queens University."

EMS changed in September of 1966 when a federal-funded report was released, entitled "Accidental Death and Disability: the Neglected Disease of Modern Society". The report, which came to be known as the 'White Paper' gave a horrific account on the impact of trauma on society. The report noted that accidents were number one cause of death for of persons between ages 1 and 37. The death rate from motor vehicle accidents had increased annually, 10,000 more in 1965 from 1964 (a 3% increase). The worst note had to be the comparison between a victim of an accident and a soldier injured in Korea. According to the White Paper, the soldier had the better chance of recovering from his injuries than the average American hurt in a car wreck. The report gave a laundry list of recommendations, including better training for field units, radio communications between ambulances and hospital emergency rooms, and the establishment of trauma systems.

R Adams Crowley (no period after the 'R'), a surgeon in Maryland, took action. He organized and set up the first freestanding trauma center, located in Baltimore, Maryland in the mid 1960's. It was Dr. Crowley who advocated the 'Golden Hour', a timeframe in which he believed the patient needed to be at the trauma center by for the best survival rate. In the late 60's, a couple of notable advanced life support (ALS) programs were started. Dr. Safar and the Freedom House Ambulance (Dr. Safar was a co-discoverer of the head-tilt/chin lift & mouth-to mouth aspects of CPR); Dr William Grace via St. Vincent Hospital (NY); Miami Fire Department (FL) under Doctors Eugene Nagle and Jim Hirschmann; and, the Los Angeles County (CA) Fire Department with Dr. Michael Criley and Dr. James Lewis at UCLA Harbor General Hospital. Doctor Leonard Cobb put together Seattle (WA)'s Medic 1 program. Patients took to the air with Flight for Life out of St. Anthony Central's Hospital in Denver (CO) in 1972. It didn't take very long for other medical flights to spring up around the country.

Dr. David R. Boyd was placed in charge of the Department of Transportation's Department of Emergency Medical Services (DEMS) by President Nixon. Dr. Boyd liked what Dr. Crowley had done with the ShockTrauma Center and wanted to expand on the idea. By the end of 1971, Dr. Boyd had set up training sessions across the USA. Despite a veto from President Nixon, Congress had passed the EMS legislation for Bill 93-154 – funding the Title 12 Administration. This allowed for the trauma hospital system, mandated emergency rooms to see patients regardless of ability to pay, and improved statistical data among other items.

Beyond the accidents, another physician, Dr. William Haddon, the Director of the National Highway Safety Bureau (NHSB) in 1969 looked at a broader picture. He knew accidents happened from three primary causes: human error, environmental, and vehicular. Dr. Haddon came up with the Haddon Matrix, which defined the accidents in the pre-accident, the accident, and post-accident phases, applying a model commonly used in the Public Health field. When he presented his Matrix, he put Emergency Medical Services at the center front, the critical piece of the system.

No longer should the public expect the stereotypical white-uniformed men in an all-white ambulance with a red cross to show up, put them on a stretcher and drive as fast as they could to drop them off at a hospital. It was Dr. Haddon's belief that the American People deserved more. In 1970, under Dr. Haddon, the NHSB became the National Highway Traffic Safety

Administration (NHTSA). Emergency Medical Services became a priority of the new department.

The National Registry of Emergency Medical Technicians (NREMT) was established in 1972 to establish standards & certifications for EMS personnel. The National Association of Emergency Medical Technicians (NAEMT) was founded in 1975 to champion the cause of EMS and Emergency Medical Services personnel. In 1979, NAEMT changed its rules, allowing non-Registry certified EMTs to join NAEMT.

Did this mean all companies jumped to upgrade equipment? No. In 1980, I worked for a company called McNulty EMS. The first ambulance I was assigned to work out of was a suburban style; a short while later, I was switched to a Cadillac-style unit and then to a low-top van. Keep in mind, the City of Los Angeles Fire Department emergency medical services (Rescue Ambulances, or RAs) were using low-top ambulances. Other companies utilized high-top vans or modular (the 'boxy-styles)) units. McNulty didn't give us portable radios.

That's right bys and girls, no hand held radios and that was not unusual for private emergency medical services. Portable radios were expensive and companies were on tight budgets. Once we stepped out of our rigs we were on our own. If, and I mean if, we were lucky the patient might have a phone in their home. Back then, many folks relied on local payphones for telephone services (the payphones could receive as well as make calls).

What is Your Emergency? The History of Public Safety Dispatching in America

Chapter Two: Attention All Units - Public Safety Embraces the Radio

"The most forward step taken since I entered the profession…"

What exactly is a radio? The Radio Club of America's member Martin Cooper writes in his article, *The Many Faces of Radio* "The term' radio' was first used around 1906, only a few years before the Radio Club of America was established, although the science and technology supporting radio dates back to at least 1873. The word 'radio' embraces any form of electromagnetic communication."

So who actually invested the radio?

The radio, or Hertzian Waves, were discovered by a man called Heinrich Rudolph Hertz. Nikola Teska and Guglielmo Marconi each claimed to develop a working radio and filed patents. Historians and experts have dabted as to which man built the first device. Tesla was credited with the discovery but history has changed and Marconi is now being given the accolade. Both men made major contributions in the field regardless of who was the 'first' to make the device work.

Radios changed the face of Public Safety forever. Before the radio was adopted by police and fire, it was being used by the military and by mainstream America for entertainment. The military communicated between ships and various units. The public airwaves broadcast news, music, and radio programs.

Reginald Fessenden is name every Public Safety employee should know. Reginald invented the modulation of radio waves as a better way to transmit weather information. He worked with Thomas Edison as a chemist for a short time until he decided to work on his own projects. Fessenden broadcast his thoughts and music over his radio in 1906. Reginald also was involved in the invention of a type of sonar called the Fessenden oscillator, utilized by submarines to locate icebergs. This device was used after the *Titanic* catastrophe in hopes of preventing another ship from colliding with an iceberg.

by Diana Sprain

The Junior Aero Club was started by a group of boys who loved flying. Two years later, those boys expanded their love of flying to the realm of wireless technology. Their new fascination included radio. Reginald was a founding member of the Junior Wireless Club Limited as a consulting engineer. The boys restructured the Aero Club to the Junior Wireless Club Limited organized on the 2nd day of January, 1909. Founding members included Harlowe Hardinge, Ernest V. Amy, Graham Lowe, Max Bamberger, Edwin Rhodes, Frank Whitehouse, L.S. Shaw, and George Burghard. These boys were to be lauded for their deep interest in amateur radio. In 1910, a bill was put before the Senate to seriously prohibit any experimentation by the lay public in the wireless realm. Senator Depew didn't count on the boys of the Radio Club. On April 28th, 1910, a committee consisting of W.E.D. Stokes, Jr., Frank King, George Eltz, and Ernest Amy pled their case before the Senate Committee on Commerce. The boys were successful. In 1911 they changed the club name to the Radio Club of America. The Radio Club of America took action in Washington a second time when the Alexander Wireless bill was put before Congress in 1912. Again, the Club members worked hard to kill the bill while it was still in committee.

The next milestone took place in 1916. Lee de Forest invented the *audion*, which is a vacuum tube that amplifies weak electric signals. Next, Lee came up with a *diode* (a variation of the audion) and then the *triode*. All of the inventions helped with the radio signals and eventually, the improvement of telephone. Charles Herrold started his radio station in 1912, although his license wasn't issued until 1921 (KQW). Herrold ran his broadcast station until 1925 (he was off the air between 1917 and 1921); later the station was sold and became KCBS out of San Francisco which is an active station to date.

On April 7th, 1921, Detroit Police Commissioner William Rutledge endorsed a little technological experimentation within the ranks of his department. He authorized one-way radio service with radios installed in the police vehicles. Commissioner Rutledge hired his nephew, Bernard 'Barney' Fitzgerald, to be the Department's first dispatcher. The transmitter was housed in the 9th

What is Your Emergency? The History of Public Safety Dispatching in America

Precinct, on the second floor in December 1922. Detroit Police Department dispatch was closed on Sundays; twenty-four hour service started in 1929. The radios worked, but as with many of the early broadcast & receive only mobile units, the system was inconsistent. To make certain the equipment functioned, the time and call sign was given every fifteen minutes. After each incident was complete, police officers had to call in to dispatch to clear the calls (they 'phoned home' long before ET made his theatrical debut).

Chicago Police came on board with radios in 1929. The initial radio traffic was done via a broadcast station status, not as a public safety licensee. Field units could get a jump on a crime within a reasonable amount of time with dispatchers putting out information over the airwaves. Convinced the electronic gadget was worth the expense, the agency installed a radio system on the 9th of August, 1930, in the main Police Headquarters where the primary switchboard was maintained.

The Federal Radio Commission (FRC) was the precursor to the Federal Communications Commission (FCC). Between official police broadcasts, the FRC mandated Detroit to play music, as the department was technically licensed as a broadcast station. In June of 1925, the Detroit Police ceased playing music. This defiance resulted in the Federal Radio Commission cancelling the KOP radio license in October of the same year. Naturally, the police department changed once the Federal Department recognized Public Safety as its own category. Detroit was issued a new license, WCK. In April of 1926 Rutledge's radio still had technical problems and went dark a year later.

Two men, patrol Officer Kenneth Cox, an electronics enthusiast, and engineering student Robert L. Batts tinkered with the radio equipment convinced radios were the key to solving crime. After seven years of builds, trials and errors, the two men were ready to install their one-way radio system. Two patrol officers, Walter Vogler and Bernard Fitzgerald teamed up with Cox spending time playing with the equipment, hoping to make improvements. The three men were issued a radio broadcast license by the Federal Radio Commission (FRC).

by Diana Sprain

In his book *Police Telecommunications*, Alan Burton included a part of a speech given by Commissioner Rutledge when he referred to the new radio system. "Eight hundred arrests with an average time of less than 90 seconds each had been made in 15 months by the radio-equipped automobiles" Commissioner Rutledge, speaking in Atlanta, proudly announced. "It is the most forward step taken since I entered the profession thirty-five years ago."

The military already used the radio to relay messages from pilots to bases or to ships. As with medical advances, the military's need spurred further research and development. The technology of radio was refined and choices expanded. As the base radio technology improved, the mobile radio changed from a one-way system to a two-way communications.

Public Safety was reluctant to grasp the emerging science at first. Visionaries in law enforcement and the fire service convinced their peers to switch to updated call response methods. Instead of signaling a field unit to find a call box and telephone a desk officer, now a patrol officer could hear information over the radio receiver. One-way radios (also called broadcast radios, because one could send out information without the ability to the listener to reply) helped improve response to crime. Dispatchers were able to provide locations of incidents in progress, suspect descriptions, or tell beat cops to call the station. Whether the field units *heard* the broadcasts was debatable, which might account for the TV show 'Car 54, Where Are You?' antics. How could the dispatchers confirm if their transmissions were copied by the field units?

The field personnel had to stop at a call box or substation to acknowledge the broadcasts. Not a very efficient system but at the time it was the only one available.

By 1930, multiple police agencies had radios in automobiles. The list included Buffalo (NY), Cincinnati (OH), Chicago (IL), Dallas (TX), Kansas City (KS), San Francisco (CA), Seattle (WA), and St Louis (MO). Berkeley and Pennsylvania had multiple stations. The City of New York even had a station for its Harbor Police.

What is Your Emergency? The History of Public Safety Dispatching in America

America was enamored with the radio. Broadcast radio was more than news programs and music. Children listened daily shows chronicling cowboys and superheroes. Housewives had on music listened as they cleaned and prepared meals, and in the evening families laughed to comedic talents of George Burns & Grace Allen; they were enthralled by sporting events; or became caught up on the daily news. One show, called *Calling All Cars* was a crime drama that featured a real Los Angeles City Police dispatcher giving a fake broadcast and the Police Chief discussing the facts of each case prior to the show commencing.

Realizing the Public Safety wasn't going away, the Federal Radio Commission issued General Order number 85 on April 8, 1930; a policy which allocated eight frequencies dedicated for police radio services. Finally, public safety had its own classification. The order required all stations in the same geographic area to operate on the same frequency, which was decided via population statistics. Michigan was issued the first state police radio system license with one-way voice communications and mobile radios. Michigan's system went live in 1930 after an extensive battle with the Washington bureaucrats. It seems no one believed there was a real need for a State law enforcement radio system. Even more so, the Federal Radio Commission had no provisions in its rules to issue any such license type. The following year, the Federal Radio Commission was still debating whether it would allow any further state-wide licenses (two additional such systems had been approved to Pennsylvania & Massachusetts); as the officials still were not convinced the license type was necessary!

Car 9, what is your location?

The one-way radio system had proved its worth. It was time for the next step. Who would be the person to change the technology for Public Safety?

That man was engineer Frank Gunther. An extraordinary individual, Frank had already touched lives with his work in radio electronics. Before working on Public Safety, Frank had worked

by Diana Sprain

with the military and even installed a receiver in one of Amelia's Earhart's planes. Frank Gunther was a man who loved his work and soon his expertise would have a major impact on Public Safety.

In Hudson County, New Jersey, the city of Bayonne was about to revolutionize the world of policing. The township of Bayonne was formed on April 1, 1861 and incorporated on March 10, 1869. In 1932, Frank Gunther was contracted to install the first two-way radios in police cars for Bayonne Police. Gunther had gone as far as to secure the first Federal Radio License (FRC) for the new Frequency Modulation (FM) band for Bayonne. The results were immediate.

Dispatchers could do more than relay information over the radio: now the field units were able to acknowledge receiving the call information. No more guessing on if the field units heard a broadcast by a dispatcher. In-progress events could be coordinated by the dispatcher, suspect descriptions broadcast to other mobile units, and block covers set up to catch bad guys who were trying to hide. Bayonne was a model department for other agencies wanting to convert to a two-way radio system.

Chiefs from other cities saw the advantages of the two-way radios. Other major cities followed suit, although many still relied heavily on call-boxes, foot patrol and mounted officers. Frank Gunther was kept busy with requests for installations. Public Safety had reached a new level of service. The era of true radio dispatching had arrived.

The first two-way State Police radio system was established by Colonel Edward J. Hickey, Commissioner of the Connecticut State Police in 1938. Connecticut's State police also had the first FM statewide installation.

The radio should be considered the most important piece of equipment, and arguably one of the most essential developments in law enforcement. Sending field units changed from a one-way affair to an interactive service. Interestingly enough, a man by the last name of Bakewell had come up with a way of transmitting photographs over the telegraph in 1847. Edouard Belin worked with Bakewell's design and improved the model. This allowed fingerprints to be shared between departments.

Dispatchers were taken from the sworn staff. Why? It could have been the 'good 'ol boy' belief that only firefighters or law enforcement personnel *knew* what they were doing. Allowing civilians to handle public safety dispatching, especially women, was unthinkable. Consider the social thinking of the early twentieth century: most women were still home-makers. Those who did work were regulated to the 'safe' jobs of secretaries, nurses, waitresses, etc. There were exceptions: August Vollmer, Chief of the Berkeley Police Department (CA), hired the first Police Woman in 1925.

Interactive radio communications allowed instant information to be passed along between dispatch and field units. Car-to-car transmissions were now possible during in-progress incidents. When a citizen contacted the station with a tip or the detectives wanted to beat cops to watch for a suspect, the dispatch could broadcast the Be-On-The Lookout (BOLO), also called an All Points Bulletin (APB) or an Attempt to Locate (ATL). Fire alarms coming in to central dispatch were now put out over the radio, as well as being toned out at the station houses. Response times to calls improved.

Radio System Basics

Police and fire departments assigned personnel to dispatch based upon need. Sometimes dispatch was stepping stone on the promotional ladder while other agencies used it as a place to put those on light duty or for personnel who some reason or another, were no longer fit to work in the field. When budget concerns necessitated field personnel return to the field, civilians were placed in dispatch.

Calls were tracked on hand written logs or data cards. Only one person could transmit at a time, while the others listened. This type of system, which is still in use in some areas, is called a Simplex system. The first dispatchers had to learn Morse code, among their police duties. Soon, the radios were configured differently, with separate frequencies for transmitting and receiving called a Duplex system. When the different frequencies are next to one another on the radio spectrum, the system is called a Full Duplex system.

What about the radio spectrum? What is the difference between UHF and 800? The UFH bands of the radio spectrum have shorter wavelengths, which make it easier for the signal to cross bad terrain or work inside buildings. The VHF band can travel further, especially during ideal conditions. The 800 band is used with a Multiplexing system. When the radio microphone is depressed, the signal searches for an open channel among the designed series of channels. A Trunked system allows simultaneous conversations to occur. The 700 bands are one another area of the radio spectrum.

The early desk microphones had two pieces that one could depress; same as many foot pedals today. As we learned, radio spectrums, or bands, are limited. Many agencies shared frequencies with other departments or even private companies such as tow or taxi cabs. Prior to transmitting, a dispatcher would push on the left-side of the microphone to make certain no one other user on the frequency was speaking. If the channel was clear, he/she could then go ahead and put out the radio traffic. For emergency calls, it might be necessary to disrupt another company's radio traffic. Hence the reason for keeping radio traffic short and to the point and breaking up long transmissions.

Head-sets were made for the military and made popular by NASA for the Space Program. Public Safety adapted the equipment for the dispatch centers. Now, dispatchers could block out background noise and concentrate on the radio. Having their hands free allowed a faster response while working in-progress incidents. Of course, there were limitations. Dispatchers could only move as far from the consoles as their cords would stretch. As head-sets improved and technology moved upward, dispatchers became more efficient. A piece of trivia: why do headsets have two prongs? One prong connects to the transmit wiring and the other to the receiving.

What is Your Emergency? The History of Public Safety Dispatching in America

Who is responsible for communications?

As more agencies jumped on the radio bandwagon, a different type of turf war developed. Just who was responsible for the purchase and upkeep of the equipment? Whose budget would pay for the communications center staff? Which agency in a city, township or county had the spare funds build the public safety building or the room to add the communications center to an existing one? Would the fire or law enforcement chief have authority over the communications center in the case of a combined dispatch? Was the expense of the radio system truly worth it?

Government pocketbooks were, and still are, tight. For single system (i.e. fire only) dispatch, communications personnel, equipment, and the dispatch center expenses were often included in the department budget. For a combined, or multiple agency communications center agency, the various chiefs had to sit down and negotiate who was paying for which expense. Often in these cases, the decision was made to split costs on a percentage basis according to usage & personnel. As for where the center was to be located, a mid-point or the agency with the biggest building was usually the best place.

Why was this important?

The hard reality of municipalities, whether it is a local city, a county, state-wide, or at the federal level, the Public Safety budget tends to make up one of the bigger part of the pie. Communications Center budgets include salaries & benefits, hiring expenses, training, equipment, equipment maintenance, office supplies, and overtime (remember people call in sick, take days off, and go off on work-related injuries/illnesses). Training doesn't just refer to the initial education of the new hire: this also includes mandated annual updates and re-certification for Emergency Medical Dispatchers (EMDs) or bi-annual re-certification for those personnel who utilize the Department of Justice NCIC/NCJIS criminal history and data files.

Another issue police and fire chiefs had to contend with was the upkeep of the radio equipment. Radio towers, repeaters,

by Diana Sprain

transceivers, and receivers all need regular maintenance. High winds, snow, rain, lightning, and mud slides could damage wiring & tower equipment. Batteries eventually wore out and had to be replaced. Radios in vehicles had to be checked: wires broke and microphones became damaged from use/abuse. Departments had no choice but to hire Technicians to handle to upkeep.

An example of how radios improved field personnel patrol performance is shown in the 1933 stats of the Los Angeles Police Department. LAPD added radios and went live in May of 1933. In the previous month of April, *before* the radios had been installed, the total number of arrests logged for the *entire* department was 550 (41 felonies). The following month the number increased, with 625 arrests (178 felonies). The difference was immediate: and the reason was communications between the dispatchers and Los Angeles Police Department's 43 radio cars exchanging information.

Radios and dispatchers had proven their worth.

Regional police communications were encouraged by the Federal Radio Commission: 35 different regional systems were in use in the mid-thirties. One of the first regional radio system placed in use was in Chicago. The equipment consisted of three transmitters in three counties and 56 agencies. Another large system was in Berkeley (CA), covering the East Bay/San Francisco Area. An example of a small regional system was Kansas City (KS), covering only 15 square miles.

In 1934, a piece of legislation called the Communications Act, did away with the Federal Radio Commission and established a new agency: the Federal Communications Commission (FCC). The Federal Communications Commission was given a wider scope of duties, taking over the telecommunications duties previously handled by the Interstate Commerce Commission. Big Brother was alive and anxious to get busy.

Contra Costa County (CA) wanted to upgrade from the one-way radio system they had as part of their membership in the Berkeley Regional Radio. Three men, George K. Burton of the Contra Costa County Sheriff's Department, Brower McMurphy of the Alameda County Sheriff, and Chief Hare of the Piedmont

What is Your Emergency? The History of Public Safety Dispatching in America

Police Department put their heads together. They filed an application with the FCC for a base station license in 1937. They were granted a license for a 30 watt station (remember, it was based on population). That would only work for a five mile radius. An automatic repeater housed on Mount Diablo would solve any transmission problems. Another application was filed, but the FCC had never received this type of request before. The FCC staff even contacted the men, telling them 'it won't work' but after some back and forth, agreed to let them try.

The experiment was a huge success. Contra Costa was able to handle their two-way traffic and more. They became a regional dispatch, adding local California Highway Patrol, county fire districts, Sonoma County, Solano County, and Lake County. Even more important, the repeater system was adopted by agencies world-wide to boost radio signals. The counties eventually broke away and formed their own 'county' dispatch systems. In V.A. Leonard's *The Police Communications System* the author states, "The continued existence of a multiplied number of semiautonomous law enforcement agencies in a single metropolitan area would seem to be incompatible with any reasonable concept of efficient police organization and administration. A 'federated' system of police protection may prove to be an acceptable alternative. Under this arrangement, a metropolitan-wide agency would join with local departments in an integrated operation designated to possess the advantages of a single metropolitan police authority and yet, not do violence to the principle of local autonomy."

Combined law enforcement agencies make sense. Instead of five training departments or six chiefs, a metropolitan agency has one. Funding can be focused on field personnel, equipment, and ancillary staff. Combined agencies also share a regional dispatch center – generally at the largest law enforcement department. Regional dispatch centers may have the fire dispatch services at the same center as the law enforcement, or at a stand-alone communications center.

Fire services learned about interoperability the hard way. Every spring into the late fall, millions of acres are lost to wildland fires. Local, state and national firefighters join together to put out the blazes and save homes. This requires a massive effort, including coordination of manpower and resources.

In 2002, the U.S. Fire Administration did a study on fire departments across the United States with over 8000 departments participating. In the communications section, a couple of key issues stood out: interoperability within local, state, or Federal agencies, fire ground communications between fire personnel and the Incident Commander, and inadequate radios used by personnel during firefighting duties. Remember, this was in 2002; eleven years later the concerns are still valid. Yes, the FCC is working to change this in as far as the interoperability concerns, but many of the other points brought up in the study have yet to be solved in many departments. The concerns in regards to ground ops communications must be improved to prevent serious injuries or loss of lives. The study reported 32.5% of fire departments had their dispatch services through local or regional law enforcement Public Safety Answering Points (PSAP) and 34.3% have dispatch via a combined (police/fire) PSAP. Only 40% of fire departments said they had a back-up dispatch facility.

The private ambulance service didn't accept the radio as easily. The initial start-up cost of applying for a license and then purchasing the actual equipment was a hurdle for many of the companies. Keep in mind that many of the smaller services were initially owned and operated by funeral homes. Other companies were operated by volunteers, with the dispatchers as the few paid employees. It was the 1950's when radios started showing up in the private ambulances, as noted by the designation 'radio-dispatched' on the side of many units. Gradually, the radio found its way inside every ambulance, along with trained medical personnel.

When Emergency Medical Services companies did get their radios, they often had to share the frequencies. Whether the dispatcher had a real base station set-up or a desk mike and a foot pedal, the procedures for dispatching were the same back in the early days. Before transmitting, one had to key up the left foot pedal (or bar on the desk mike) and make sure no one else was

What is Your Emergency? The History of Public Safety Dispatching in America

talking. If it was quiet, one could then put out whatever radio traffic needed and end it with the time and your FCC call sign using the right-side foot pedal (or desk mike section). If another company was talking, the dispatcher had to wait – or, if you could break in and ask them to hold off for your emergency traffic. When the school buses and cab were moved to other band widths, public safety agencies across the country all did happy dances.

At McNulty, we shared a frequency with a local school bus company. After hours, we had the channel to ourselves. Imagine trying to dispatch a medical call in between the "Mrs. Smith said Benny wasn't picked up" conversations.

"I don't want to carry this cumbersome radio thing around with me!"

The second biggest innovation to slap public safety upside the head was the handheld transceiver, or portable radio. The credit of this vital piece of equipment has been accredited to different people: Donald Hings, Aldred Gross, or the Motorola Company engineers (Dan Noble, Raymond Yoder, Henryk Magnuski, Marion Bond, Lloyd Morris, and Bill Vogel). Regardless of which of the inventors, no one could diminish the importance of the handheld transceiver. Portable radios, also called Handie-Talkies, handheld, X-Units, or Mobiles, were developed during the time of the Second World War. The original radio handsets were large and cumbersome, and carried in backpacks or shoulder bags. With advances in science engineers were able to make the portable radios smaller, therefore adaptable for Public Safety use.

Law enforcement was the first of the three major branches to adopt the hand-held radios. Demonstrations at conventions showed how a portable radio could improve officer safety. Department heads gradually realized the potential benefits of the device, purchasing the radios for their patrol officers. Fire departments were slow to add the new portable radios to their equipment. The general feeling at the time among firemen was that the men knew how to do their jobs: providing field personnel with the handheld radios wouldn't make any difference.

by Diana Sprain

This mindset took years to change in the medical community. Emergency Medical Service agencies were the last of the three branches to join the base station radio bandwagon and they were just as slow to jump on the portable radio train. Before emergency medical service agencies added hand-held radios, they had bigger issues to conquer, mainly medical standards of their field personnel. The Emergency Medical Services community eventually fixed both issues.

As far as the late 1980's, there were Emergency Medical Service companies that sent out crews to calls without portable radios. Once the Emergency Medical Technicians stepped out of their ambulance, their only means of communications was a telephone, if the patient was near one. I can recall multiple instances of exiting the unit with my partner in areas of Oakland that the police wouldn't go in without back-up, in the dark because street lights were broken while crossing our fingers that we'd make it back to the ambulance. Unless a caller said the complaint for for a complaint deemed an emergency, the fire department didn't respond. Needless to say, that stomach ache often turned out to be due to a stabbing, the 'don't feel good' was due to an overdose, and the patient with back pain had been shot. It's a wonder we survived our shifts. Eventfully, the company began issuing portable radios and many of the crews purchased Kevlar vests for personal protection.

At least the Paramedic crew had a 'biophone' option (also referred to as 'the anchor' due to its weight of 60 pounds). Another piece of equipment used by the first paramedics was a portable electrocardiograph (ECG or EKG) transmitter. Today, crews do much of their communications via cellular telephones.

Chapter Three: Civilians Take Over

Uniforms belong on the streets

Who can say when the moment actually happened? Did a sergeant wander in to the radio room, half a stogie clamped in his mouth, a cup of coffee gripped in one hand, and stare at the uniform officer sitting at the radio? Finally growling a "Who's available? Mrs. Dougherty's husband and brother are fighting again."

"Sorry, Sarge, I only have George, and I can't send him by himself. You know those two always end up in a knock-down, drag-out fight. Unless you want to go with George…or, you can take over the radio and I'll go. Otherwise it will have to hold up until a cover unit is available." A few choice swear words pour out of the sergeant's mouth as he ponders which way to handle the call.

Regardless of the dispatchers rank (sworn or non-sworn), it became an unwritten rule that the person operating the radio was the 'voice' of the department. One can even take it a step further, as I was told during my probation with the police, and claim that the radio dispatcher is 'the voice of the Chief'. Initially in the communications center, firefighters and law enforcement officers handled the radio responsibilities. Phone calls were transferred to the call-taking room where information was collected. After determining the problem, the radio dispatchers sent out field personnel to handle the incidents. Persons who came directly to the station spoke to desk officers, who in turn, referred the victims to the appropriate detective division. Those who showed up at fire stations talked to whoever answered the door.

A common proverb is "The chain is no stronger than the weakest link." This is especially true in Public Safety. Dispatchers must be enabled to perform the job by the administrators and the communications center managers. Without appropriate policies & procedures (P&Ps) in place, dispatch personnel are relegated to being glorified parrots over the radio. If an agency wants a patrol or fire supervisor to be in complete charge, that is fine.

by Diana Sprain

Unfortunately, this method wastes valuable time in emergencies. General Orders, combined with dispatch-specific policies & procedures, allow dispatchers to make instant decisions and manage in-progress incidents without waiting for supervisor approval.

Once the pendulum had swung to civilians, administrators had to decide on a job title for the dispatch staff. In the early days of professional Telecommunicators, there were no set standards for duties or training. Common job titles included radio officer, dispatcher-clerk, signal officer, radio-dispatcher, and operator among others. Dispatchers argued to have the 'clerk' removed from the job title, as they felt it was an affront to be looped in with the clerical pool. Even today, our sisters and brothers are working to have the federal government move our job classification out of the general clerical section and in to the public safety/first responder category. It seems no one in the federal government really knows what Public Safety Telecomunicators really do.

The question of sworn verses non-sworn was debated all the way up to the 70's, as illustrated in Alan Burton's treatise, *Police Communications*, "Should policemen be employed as dispatchers when there is no anticipated need to exercise the police powers of arrest? If there is such public contact, it should be with a policeman with several years of field experience."

That certainly can be up for discussion when many agencies are small enough to have dispatch personnel monitor front counters and assist visitors between phone calls and radio traffic. Communications center personnel could be hired due to nepotism. Recall Detroit Police's first dispatcher, Bernard 'Barney' Fitzgerald, was nephew to the Police Commissioner.

Was the change of communications staff from sworn to non-sworn simply a common sense move or could it have been a change made due to a budget reasons? Looking back, why have a perfectly healthy, capable patrolman or firefighter sit in dispatch when that same person could be out in the field? Hire civilians, train each man or woman to the skill level desired, and keep the field personnel running calls. Oh, and let's pay those dispatchers less money. Regardless of the reason, law and fire departments gradually made the switch and were generally pleased with the results.

Even with the change of call-takers and dispatcher from sworn to non-sworn, supervisors continued to be those with badges in many agencies. When I started at Berkeley, all of the shift supervisors were sworn police officers and we had a fire captain in dispatch as well. Later, the fire captain was replaced by a fire lieutenant and the sworn supervisors replaced by non-sworn overseen by a sworn. Eventually the sworn manager was replaced by a civilian. We proved we could handle our own.

Switchboard Operator to Radio Dispatcher

There may have been one person within any given agency who was a logical choice for the 'new' dispatcher position: the department switchboard operator. He, or she, was taking phone calls and routing each request throughout the agency. The operator had to perform a quick assessment of the caller's need prior to making the transfer to the appropriate division and/or individual.

The new 'Dispatchers' did become items of news. Kathleen Battle wrote about the Mason City Police Department in her book, "Calling All Cars". After the Mason City Police Department installed their radio system and hired full-time dispatchers, the City placed receivers in offices of the police chief, the police captain, the fire department, and the city manager. The local newspaper frequently ran stories about the dispatch center complete with photographs.

The telephone had been adopted by public safety, especially the law enforcement agencies. Telephones allowed two-way communications, not just in the method of reporting crime, but also in the initial response to incidents. With a telephone system, agencies could pass on information to other departments within the county, state or even across the nation.

V.A. Leonard, in his book, *"The Police Communications System"* gives an example of how the telephone system helped capture a homicide suspect. "On the evening of September 2, 1889, Walter Koeller, lying sick in his room in an East Chicago Boarding house, was stabbed to death by two young men who had called upon him. The landlord, startled by the cries of the victim, ran from the house in search of a policeman, but when she returned with an officer a few minutes later, the murderers had fled. The officer rushed to a patrol box and notified his station of the crime, providing a good description of the assassins which the landlady had given him, and mentioned the fact that one of them carried a suitcase."

"The information, including the descriptions of the two men and the nature of their crime, was given by headquarters to every precinct station in the city, so that less than an hour from the time of the murder, it was known in all stations. This information in turn, was given to every police officer on duty, when he called in to make his hourly report."

"At eleven o'clock, an officer arrested in a rail yard two suspects who answered the descriptions, and a few hours later, Inspector Shea of the Detective Division, had a full confession of the murder. Thus, by means of a new communications facility, a crime was cleared which might have remained a mystery, for had the men succeeded in leaving Chicago, it is probable that they would ever have been apprehended."

Alan Burton explains the authority of the dispatcher by quoting O.W. Wilson, "…the giving of orders by an agent who has no authority in his own right, but who performs the routine tasks of command as a service for his principal."

The early civilian dispatchers had an easy time going through the hire process. Employees were hired on reputations, because of fathers, brothers, or other family members already working in the department, or after a quick interview with the chief. Depending on the size of the agency, the new dispatcher might have a short on-the-job orientation to the radio equipment, or spend a little time with a tenured dispatcher. Quite a difference from the seemly endless hoops of red tape a perspective dispatch candidate goes through today. It's a daunting task even discovering when the jobs are available today. Does one look at the agency website, a newspaper (assuming local papers still exist, a state site, any one of a dozen private job sites).

What is Your Emergency? The History of Public Safety Dispatching in America

Glendale Police Department hired its first dispatcher, Virgil Glidden, in 1949. Until then, Glendale PD utilized the red light mounted on top of a water tower to signal patrol officers to call in when an incident was pending, even *after radios were installed in the patrol vehicles.* Glendale PD's radio system was put in service in 1940.

Departments were encouraged to look for certain traits in their dispatch staff. Personal discipline, a strong work ethic, accuracy in the job, and knowledge of the response area were desired in potential candidates. The ability to think quickly, to be able to perform more than one task at a time (multi-tasking), to use a computer, to read a map, to take information in an expeditious manner, possess common sense, and be able to remain calm in a crisis were, and still are, important traits in communication center personnel. Prior radio and/or field experience was a plus.

One solution was to hire police cadets to work the radio room. This would give the Police Chief an endless supply of enthusiastic personnel willing to do a good job for little or no pay. The same went for the Fire Chief, using potential firefighters. The only problem with cadets was the limited time in dispatch. Once the cadet or student firefighter finished college, he certainly didn't want to stay working in dispatch.

Dispatch Centers were expected to be organized from the moment information was first gathered from the reporting person to the time it was given to the officer, who per V.A. Leonard, "The complainant is untrained in police technique and at the moment if reporting a crime, particularly a serious one, he is emotionally unstable...requires expert coaching in order to get from him without delay the facts..."

Personnel recruited had to be tough. The new dispatchers were working with old-time field personnel who were used to being independent. Many of the law enforcement officers started out before radios were used. These cops worked alone, only calling for help in the worst of situations. Firefighters relied on the other guys in their station. The desk officers were *one of them.* Civilians had no idea what it was like in the streets; how could civilian dispatchers get it right? How could a civilian understand the danger a cop or firefighter might face on a call – especially a *woman*, who didn't even work in the field.

Duties for the early dispatchers were varied from what they are now. Many of those groundbreakers came from secretarial pools, and still performed various mundane chores such as making coffee for the station, cleaning common areas, and delivering mail through-out the building. Other duties included searching female prisoners, processing bond paperwork, filing warrants, taking messages, and babysitting juveniles. Of course, the dispatch personnel took phone calls for complaints.

"She is aware she may not advance and is therefore content…"

The size of an agency dictates how it is divided up for administration and to whom each division is accountable. Small agencies may not break up to divisions at all, or may have their department separated as operations (field personnel), ancillary service (non-field personnel) and, administration. Dispatch would often be placed under the ancillary service section. A medium size department might break up sworn personnel in to various divisions. Dispatch would become part of the operations or service section in this case. A large department would have multiple divisions, with Dispatch under its own bureau.

When the Communications Center made the switch from sworn police officers & firefighters, to civilian dispatchers many agencies still left a uniformed officer in charge. Sworn personnel, ranked anywhere from Sergeants to Lieutenants, would oversee the day-to-day operations of dispatch. Scheduling, complaint investigations, and general everyday management would be handled by the uniformed personnel. In some cases, both a firefighter and a law enforcement officer co-supervised. They were responsible for writing the Communications Center policies and procedures, even if said persons never actually put on a headset or answered a telephone call! Management felt supervisors didn't need to know how to perform the job to write the job's policies.

Many dispatchers would debate this reasoning.

What is Your Emergency? The History of Public Safety Dispatching in America

Dispatch staffing wasn't proportional to field personnel. Depending on the agency, dispatch staffing varied from one all the way to over 100. It stands to reason the larger the department, the more the department would break down the jurisdiction to different zones, each with its own radio channel. Along with 'normal' channels, larger agencies would set aside 'tactical' channels for in-progress incidents (or special events, high-risk warrant services, etc), car-to-car channels, inquiry requests (license plate checks, warrant checks etc.), a mutual aid channel, and a channel for secondary requests (tows, phone calls, misc information checks, etc). Fire departments would have a similar breakdown of needs: everyday channel to dispatch units, a tactical channel or two (for working fires), a channel for EMS (or for use in a major incident), and a mutual aid channel. Alas, the smaller agencies had to get by with less: less radio channels, smaller quantities of field units, and fewer communications center personnel.

Many agencies used communications systems similar to this for decades. Once Computer-Aided Dispatch (CAD) systems along with computerized phone and digital radios arrived on the scene, dispatch set-ups like this one disappeared. Sadly, the knowledge of the personnel who worked in these communications centers was irreplaceable. No one knew the jurisdictions like the 'old style' dispatchers.

During the early years of civilian dispatchers, a bias was apparent. Women were preferred over men. Why was this so? Alan Burton believed the reasons were obvious, when looking back and considering society's way of thinking. He noted in his *Police Telecommunication*: "…There is seldom a shortage of women seeking jobs. Women will often do the same work as a man but for less money…she is aware she may not advance and is therefore content."

This was a sexist mindset but one must consider that this text was written in 1973. Alan also wrote that women didn't know the streets as well as men, "with virtually no chance of gaining this valuable experience." At the time, I guess he didn't think women ever left the house or were capable of reading a map. He went on, claiming women required special conditions, including a limit of hours that could be worked in a day (due to family obligations) and a couch (so they could rest).

In a later edition of *Police Telecommunications,* the sexist remarks were removed. I think Alan's female co-workers scolded him after reading his book and demanded the offending remarks be changed. An officer once told me he preferred female dispatchers on the radio because he could distinguish a woman's voice quicker over the radio than a man's in a crisis. During that particular time the amount of female officers to male officers (and male to female dispatchers) was small in that particular department. Was that a true statement, this author can't say; however the police officer stood firm on his belief. The profession seems to be female dominated. Is it a stigma for men to be behind a radio instead of out on the street? Maybe some day a PhD will do a study on this and answer that question.

When I first started at Berkeley PD, the communications center was located in a windowless room on the third floor of an ancient building. How old? It was used in a Hollywood pilot for a police drama set in the 40's (50's?). One could picture an old-style detective, a cigar clamped between his teeth, walking in a crook to the squad room to be questioned.

The dispatch center used small 'IBM" cards to record calls and status of units. Dispatchers rotated positions (call-taker, fire radio, police radio) on an irregular basis. A long belt went the length of the room separated in three sections (the middle went backwards and the other two went forward to the radio positions: one to police and the other to the fire). Two huge glass-covered maps of the city, one with the fire districts and the other with the police beats were at the front of the corresponding radio stations. Each had enough slots with linked lights on the maps. Flip a switch and a light turned on: green for in-service (or available) and red for out-of-service (or on a call). A desk held the time stamping machine and a foot pedal was underneath. A Centracomm console with all available radio channels, an intercom, and other bells & whistles was under the map. The call-taking positions and record-keeping (we typed out the daily police and fire logs) were separated by a flimsy wall with Plexiglas windows. The walls were

What is Your Emergency? The History of Public Safety Dispatching in America

covered with a thick cloth, which let us pin memos and maps up. It was a basic set-up but it worked. For in-progress calls, we'd write on the glass with a grease pencil. It was fantastic for marking out block covers.

Departments can work short-staffed due to a myriad of reasons, including personnel out on work-related injuries, positions open due to resignations, and hiring freezes. For example, one administrator's solution to help out a dispatch center chronically short-handed was to allow dispatch trainees to work, without being monitored by their trainers, up to the capacity to which each individual had been trained. If the trainee had passed the fire dispatch phase, then the trainee was allowed to work a call taking or the fire dispatch position (having completed phase one - call taking and phase two - fire dispatch). In addition, non-dispatch personnel were trained as call takers and/or radio dispatchers for either fire or police. These 'specialty' personnel were limited in when they could work, that way the regular staff on duty wasn't overburdened with too many 'specialty' position and not enough regular dispatch personnel. The non-dispatch personnel allowed to train as specialty overtime were police officers and police service assistants. The department also contracted with a temporary help agency and trained a limited amount of clerical personnel as call-takers.

Was this a good idea or a bad one? The temporary agency staff had to pass a background, and all non-dispatcher personnel had to go through limited training program for the positions to which they would work. The supervisors had a nightmare when it came to staffing. Only so many limited skills personnel were allowed per shift, even when the restricted skills folks were willing to work. When needed, fully-trained dispatch staff were ordered to work via mandatory overtime in order to cover the police & warrant channels. The few police officers who initially volunteered soon changed their minds when they discovered each of them was expected to work the police radio.

Private Emergency Medical Services had been using civilian dispatchers since the service started. The smaller mom & pop companies relied on family members or clerical staff to act as

by Diana Sprain

dispatchers. As the companies grew, regular full-time dispatch personnel were hired. In many cases, Emergency Medical Service agencies hired Emergency Medical Technicians or paramedics to work the radios, with the thinking that their medical training would be a plus when handling the phones. The field personnel's training & experience did not always translate well to answering phone calls or dealing with a hysterical person. The issue of liability came up when there was no specific program in place and the Emergency Medical Service personnel were 'winging it' with callers.

Not all agencies went to civilians. Some departments went back and forth.

The County of Los Angeles Fire Department started out with civilian fire dispatchers. In the early 1970's, the decision was made to switch back to uniformed fire personnel. The safety service personnel worked a twenty-four hour shift (known as a 'Kelley' schedule, or ten days a month), just as the fire station staff did. There were initially multiple satellite dispatch centers. The Communications Center worked with up to five dispatchers, plus a Fire Captain. Administration made a decision to switch back to civilian dispatchers in 1992, and the smaller satellite centers were gradually been phased out as well.

The City of San Francisco (CA) was manned by volunteers up until a series of fires in 1850. The City leaders called a meeting and appointed the Police Chief to organize a fulltime fire department. The first order of business was to acquire equipment. Volunteers kept the force going until the paid personnel were hired. The telegraph office was staffed 24 hours a day once the alarm boxes were hooked up. According to a copy of a news article on the San Francisco Fire Department website, the alarms came in on a piece of tape. The tape recorded alarm boxes via a Morse code-like system of dots, dashes, and spaces. The alarm box operators would match the combination of the symbols to a box and strike out the bells to warn fire companies of incidents.

San Francisco Fire Department's alarm center was destroyed in the 1906 earthquake. The alarm center had been staffed by firefighters and after the new alarm center was rebuilt, the personnel kept their jobs. Dispatchers tracked fire companies using a peg board and card system. That changed when the Department upgraded to a Computer-Aided Dispatch system (CAD). The Fire and Department of Public Health dispatch services merged to a consolidated Public Safety Answering Point (PSAP) in 2000, spearheaded by San Francisco Fire Chief Joanne Hayes-White. Firefighters initially moved to the new communications center, but were replaced by civilian dispatchers.

Can you understand me now? Plain talk verses radio codes.

To speak in code or not is a decision each agency had to decide as radios were added. When law enforcement departments first acquired radios, they shared the air waves with other commercial broadcasters and/or other departments. The spectrum was crowded, with limited availability. Radio transmissions needed to be short and to the point, hence the development of codes.

The codes gave an air of professionalism. Once scanners were invented, and available for the public, the radio codes kept the conversations cryptic. Of course, that changed once code lists became public knowledge. For those listening in on scanners, the key for every agency's codes became a necessity. The Radio Shack Corporation published a soft cover book for years which had lists of radio call signs, radio frequencies, and a basic ten code list. Regardless of any published lists, there are no real standard radio codes, as Alan Burton in his *Communications Guide for Public Safety Dispatchers* notes: "Of all the signal lists in use by police departments, a very small percentage claim to be "universal" versions. Of these, one lists 58 code signals, another 68, and a third numbers 119 codes (not counting statute section numbers used to supplement the universal code). Of all those professing to use the "universal" code, all agreed on only eight signals. The eight signals found to be in consistent common usage are:

    10-4   message received

10-7   out of service
10-8   in service
10-9   repeat your message
10-20 what is your location
10-22 cancel
10-28 registration check
10-29 check for wanted

    Alan then explains how radio codes can be found in the 900-series, 10-hundred series, 11-hundred series, and how many departments also use criminal, vehicle, state, and city & county ordinance codes. An example of the disparity between law enforcement officers calling in an emergency call for help exists in the Southwest. Looking at four different agencies, two in California and two in Nevada, the codes are as follows: 940b, 1199, 444, and Code Red. The two California and two Nevada agencies are in conjoining jurisdictions. Even a simple on scene is confusing: with a 10-23 or 1097. Is it any wonder law enforcement agencies are gradually moving to plain talk?

    Call identification numbers have evolved over the decades. Law enforcement units were initially known by their individual badge (or shield) numbers; that changed as field personnel staffing increased and computer-aided dispatch software was developed. The trend in law enforcement was to divide cities or counties in to beats and to assign patrol officers to the beats. Officers took on beat identifiers (1A12) instead of their badge (or shield) number.

    Emergency Medical Services has been a mixed bag on whether it uses codes or not. A company may go along with county guidelines, using limited codes on their personal channel and plain-talk on the mutual channels. Fire service traditionally keeps to a plain-talk style, staying away from any codes. The Incident Command System (ICS), and its cousin the National Incident Management System (NIMS), stipulate common English instead of any codes be used in all communications to prevent misunderstandings.

What is Your Emergency? The History of Public Safety Dispatching in America

A home away from home: the communications center

Dispatch centers vary as much as radio demeanor & codes. Small agencies or departments might have a radio near the front counter or at a clerical person's desk. Others have designated communication centers within public safety building or even stand-alone dispatch centers.

A properly designed communications center has a break room, also referred to as a 'quiet room', for the communications center staff to get away from the radios and telephones. After handling a tough radio incident or telephone call a telecommunicator or call-taker may need to take a moment to clear their head. Dispatch personnel prefer to have meal breaks away from the consoles (unless they work in a single telecommunicator center). A nice break facility includes a television, a microwave, a refrigerator, a couch, and a full bathroom with a shower. This is a necessary part of the planning for a dispatch area. In the event of a major event, mandatory overtime (when a co-worker calls off sick in the last minute), or bad weather the dispatchers may not be able to leave. Having the ability to meet their basic needs will go a long way to make the Telecommunications employees happy, especially when the dispatchers may not be able to leave the confines of the communications center for extended period of times.

The communications center must have a generator back-up set to go on in the event of a power failure. All computers and other telecommunications equipment should have UPS back-ups. Basic supplies should be stored within easy access, including water, food, cots, blankets, flashlights & batteries, and first aid material for the Telecommunicators use.

Are all dispatch centers nice and cozy? No. One dispatch I worked at had a terrible rodent problem that required a company cat to kill the mice. Another one had a similar problem. It was a nasty feeling when you'd be in the middle of a phone call and feel a creature run over your shoes. We put out spring-traps to catch the mice. When one went off, we'd argue about who had to dispose of the dead mouse. I didn't miss *those* rooms when we moved.

by Diana Sprain

Chapter Four: Public Safety Gets Organized

Police Chiefs make their own radio rules

Single incidents are easy enough to handle by the desk officers and fire alarm operators. Major incidents or disasters present unique problems. The event can quickly overwhelm the system. Whether it is a wildland fire, hurricane, tornado, earthquake, or riot, the call-boxes or one-way radio, the challenges of coordinating response via radio can be a headache. As we have seen with our modern critical events, too many people trying to talk on limited channels at the same time, the possibility of phone service crashes, or even the dispatch center rendered unfit can impact the public safety system. After the two-way radios took the place of the call-boxes & one-way systems, the public started to demand more bang for their tax buck.

The radio room personnel, field units, and the public weren't connecting. Fire had their protocols, law enforcement had procedures, and ambulances had little training. All persons involved in the business of saving lives and property agreed 'something' had to be done. What they couldn't agree on was how to fix the problems. Administrators pointed fingers at one another in all directions during meetings and conferences. No one wanted to take responsibility. The press was grinning with delight over the chaos: major wild land fires were killing firefighters, cops were doing their own thing, and EMS was still in the 'grab and go' stage rarely saving people.

In the early days of the twentieth century, the modern police and fire professions were in their infancy when it came to communications technology. The good ol boy system of 'you scratch my back and I'll scratch yours' existed. Rules and regulations were being made up as situations dictated. Federal agencies were trying to anticipate future needs, but technology was moving too fast. Government had a habit of stepping in and stirring the pot, writing regulations on a kneejerk basis not always thinking the wording through, often relying on input from commercial sources for guidance. Public Safety agencies didn't want Big

What is Your Emergency? The History of Public Safety Dispatching in America

Brother regulating them to death, but changes were needed. Various national agencies put out scathing reports slamming public safety on the handling of incidents in general, with specific mention of communications as it related to field personnel. Different United States Presidents assigned task forces to study areas of public safety and report back with areas to be improved.

Crime rates in the metropolitan cities grew along with the population. If one believed the newspaper headlines, government was corrupt. Was the soaring violence propaganda or actual facts? After the stock market crash caused the Great Depression and left 25% of the USA's residents unemployed, many people who lacked the basic necessities in life turned to crime. It was simple, a family needed to eat. To get food, breadwinners stole to feed their families, but petty theft was not the same as robbery or homicide. The rising crime rate was a concern to the law enforcement community at all levels.

President Lyndon Johnson appointed a multiple group task force to study law enforcement and crime. The members were broken up to different task forces, each assigned different areas of concern. When the committees finished the research and published their report, no one in law enforcement was surprised by the results. Any resident of the inner cities could have told Johnson's appointees what the problems were. The task force report started with a basic description of the communications problem. "The primary input to the command and control system, and the most frequent initiator of the apprehension process, is a call from a citizen, usually a victim of a crime or a witness. In the case of street crimes, however, it is often difficult for the victim or a witness to call the police promptly. A number of things can be done to improve existing street communications equipment to make it easier to reach the police."

"Police call-boxes should be designated 'public emergency call-boxes', should be better marked and lighted, and should not be locked…" The report also noted "When trying to call the police from an ordinary telephone, a person is faced with a bewildering array of police jurisdictions and associated telephone numbers…Whenever practical, a single number shoulder be established, at least within a metropolitan area and preferably over the entire United States, comparable to the telephone company's long-distance information number. This is difficult but feasible with existing telephone switching centers; it appears more practical with the new electronic switching system being installed by the telephone companies, and should be incorporated. In the interim, the telephone companies should print on each telephone number disc the number of the police department serving that telephone's location."

A response to the task force report by Dennis Flannery in a letter dated 21 December, 1967 (as catalogued in the LBJ Presidential Library) stated the problem of frequency congestion was partly to blame for the law enforcement problems. He suggested the amount of radio traffic made for a shortage of frequency space, which led to extended response times. Mr. Flannery mentioned the Communications Center specifically, "Overtaxing of central police dispatchers during normal peak hours of operation, such as Friday and Saturday evenings." He went on to list other items that caused a reduced response to crime, including units having to wait to update status on radios and inhibition of development of personnel radio systems (portables) which connect officers to headquarters.

Who's watching over us?

In 1934, a new Federal department, the Federal Communications Commission, was established by the Communications Act on June 19th, 1934, to replace the Federal Radio Commission. This new agency followed a series of predecessors, including the Interstate Commerce Commission; Radio Service division of the Bureau of Navigation (Dept. of Commerce and Labor); and, the Department of State – licensing of submarine cable operations. Needless to say, these prior departments came from a wide range of areas.

The Federal Communications Commission was tasked with jurisdiction over the telecommunications industry in addition to the radio world. The agency was set up to receive its funding from

What is Your Emergency? The History of Public Safety Dispatching in America

regulatory fees. The Commission is overseen by five Commissioners, who are appointed by the President of the United States, and confirmed by the United States Senate. These Commissioners serve a term of five years, unless they are chosen to fill for a short-term appointment. Congress did set a check & balance for the FCC Commissioners: only three may be of the same political party and none of them are allowed to have any financial interest in any FCC-related business.

There are a few bureaus and offices within the Federal Communications Commission's particular interest to Public Safety Telecommunications: the Enforcement Bureau, the Consumer and Governmental Affairs Bureau, the Public Safety & Homeland Security Bureau, the Office of Engineering & Technology, the Office of the Inspector General, and the Office of Legislative Affairs.

As it implies, the Enforcement Bureau handles 'policing' of the Communications Act, FCC rules, terms, and contracts of authorizations. The Consumer & Governmental Affairs does much of the same for the Public. This bureau also is involved in emergency preparation and new technologies. Public Safety and Homeland Safety handles all matters related to emergency services including 911, interoperability, Disaster Information Clearing House, Master PSAP Registry, Network Outage Reporting System, and licensing. The Office of Engineering & Technology handles radio spectrum allocation. This office has a Federal Communications Commission ID tool search just in case someone wanted to look up an agency call sign. The Office of the Inspector General provides reports, press releases and helpful information. Finally, the Office of Legislative Affairs lists meetings dates, meeting minutes, and correspondence from the Commissioners.

American Telephone & Telegraph (AT&T) for many years held a monopoly on the phone market. In the 1960's, AT&T was challenged by MCI, who offered lower rates for long distance services. The Federal Communications Commission allowed more telephone companies to enter the long distance business. Eventually, this led to an anti-trust lawsuit by the Justice Department in 1982 which resulted in the breakup of "Ma Bell".

by Diana Sprain

The Courts ruled that the AT&T had to grant access to their hard lines to other phone companies for long distance access. With the breakup of AT&T, the door was held wide open for anyone to offer telephone service. Would internet and VoIP service have happened, or occurred at least as quickly, had AT&T stayed in one piece? One can only speculate.

Smokey's Not Amused

Wildland fires have always been feared by those who have chosen to live outside of any metropolitan area. After Theodore Roosevelt established the National Parks System, a serious look was directed at wildland fires. In 1885, the first forest fire control program was established in the Adirondacks Reserve, and a second program instituted in Yellowstone the following year. Both Parks had based their control management operations plan on a similar format developed in West Germany. The fire prevention design was simple: try to prevent fires in the first place and put out any that start as quickly as possible.

In 1933, a wildland fire called the Tillamok Burn destroyed 3 million acres. After the ashes had cooled, the National Parks policy changed. Personnel were directed to put out any fire before 10:00 am. How could any fire department guarantee a fire could be extinguished by a certain time? To start, the National Parks had a pool of fresh-faced young adults eager to help. A new organization the Civilian Conservation Corps (CCC), gave the National Forest Service a boost of emergency service personnel. As expected, the policy was flawed but the forest fire management policy endured until 1976.

Even in the wetlands of the Florida Everglades, fire management was problematic. In Hal K. Rothman's book, *Blazing Heritage – A History of Wildland Fire in the National Parks*, he writes: "By the 1950's, the National Park Service had seen enough fire at the Everglades to recognize that conditions there challenged it's assumptions about fire control. Its first crisis came in 1950, when three large fires, called Tamiami fire #3, Long Pine Key fire

#3, and Mowry fire, required simultaneous suppression. The park lacked the resources to fight all three fires at the same time.

The "fire emergency merely spotlighted this fact," Dan Beard stated in the aftermath of a critique held at Park headquarters. Beard wrote that the Park personnel showed strength in "the spirit of the men and women (permanent, seasonal, and temporary) who tackled the undertaking."…These fires clearly showed the park's technical capabilities were inadequate. The combination of information and mechanization which characterized the era had not yet reached the Everglades and the Park had not yet developed a fire management plan. Park maps were old and outdated, without roads, trails, and in some cases, terrain and plant distribution. Firefighters started with inaccurate information...The Park's communication system also fell short. Dependant on walkie-talkies as a result of absent phone lines, the park did not own enough radios set to assure constant communications, and what radios they had lacked sufficient range. Dispatchers lacked training for fire management…"

In 1957, the Chief of the U.S. Forest Service, Fire Division wanted to review why devasting wildfires occured and the impact of the department in terms of life and property loss. In prior years, wildland fires had taken a tremendous toll on firefighters. One out of control blaze at Griffith Park, Los Angeles, California in 1933, killed 25 firefighters; and the previous year in the Mendocino National Forest in California, 15 firefighters were killed fighting the Rattlesnake Fire. The Mann Gulch fire in Helena, Montana in 1949 killed 13 firefighters. The property damages were terrible but that was nothing compared to the men killed by the flames. Something had to give.

The U.S. Forest Service Fire Chief wanted answers. What could be done to prevent fatalities, reduce damages, and help prevent financial loss caused by wildland fires? Was a change in procedures needed?

A federal task force was assembled. The members of the task force spent two years gathering data and interviewing field personnel, administration staff, dispatchers, and victims. They reviewed thousands of documents. The task force spoke to trainers and tower personnel. After the investigation was over, the hard work of sorting through the data began. The committee took their time before issuing their report. The task force listed several areas of concerns, based on a critical hindsight look. The members determined various factors which seemed to be significant. Of no surprise, communications was listed as topic number five out of twelve. The notation in reference to communications said "not available, not used, or broke."

According to the report: " *Recommendation*: Give increased attention to communication on campaign fires, including exploring the use of transistor-type receivers, and encouraging the practice that receivers on all radios used on a fire line on a campaign fire be "on" at all times. One of the threads that run through the action on most of the tragedy fires (and also on fires that merely got big) is breakdown of plans for communication on the line, or inadequacy of such communication. In some cases, the breakdown may involve not having communication facilities in use during a critical period of five minutes or less. This subject requires continuing attention, but there are things that can be done now to emphasize this critical item. At least one region follows a practice that radios issued to fire line personnel on campaign fires have the receivers "on" until the sets are returned to camp. All administrative units should go at least this far."

The committee came up with a set of ten recommendations, entitled '*the ten standard fire orders*' to be used in firefighter training and later in wildland fire situations. The ten 'orders' included fire behaviors, fire line safety, and, organizational control. Later, eighteen more 'watch-out' situations were added. These became known as the '10 and 18' rules.

13 years later, in 1970, during a period of 13 days, 700 structures were destroyed and 16 lives were lost in California. Once the ashes had cooled the Powers That Be gathered together to evaluate the fire. How could the fire service improve its efforts the next time, for all agreed a conflagration of that magnitude *would* happen again, and what issues caused the biggest headaches? All involved agencies agreed two main factors were the problem: communications and cooperation.

What is Your Emergency? The History of Public Safety Dispatching in America

The Federal Government acknowledged the concerns, and the 92nd Congress delegated the U.S. Forest Service to design a system that could be used by the department to coordinate multiple agencies in fire events. The Forest Service worked with the California Fire Marshall, and the California Office of Emergency Services (OES) to come up with a new system of incident management. That system was called Firefighting Resources Organized for Potential Emergencies, or FIRESCOPE. It is still in use to day to manage wide scale fire events in California.

FIRESCOPE was heralded as a great method of fire scene management. The program was more than a tool for fire ground operations; it also was useful for other incidents. FIRESCOPE became the foundation of the next step in fire ground scene management. The Incident Command System, or ICS, was touted as the future of fire department incident management. It took time, but eventually the fire community accepted Incident Command System as the normal event handling mode. ICS evolved further when the system branched out and became the National Incident Management System (NIMS), to handle major national events, typically of the disaster-level size. In 1974, the National Wildfire Coordinating Workgroup NWCW) was established to oversee federal and state fire management programs.

FIRESCOPE didn't go away. Part of FIRESCOPE's acceptance and continued use to this day alongside Incident Command System (ICS) is the program's ease of use for any size fire but the Incident Command System is adaptable to any type of event. The technical team adopted common terminology for the Incident Command System in 1976. In 1978, agencies were encouraged to use ICS for every call handled, no matter how small. The Los Angeles Fire Department led the way by formally accepting ICS for everyday use. California Department of Forestry (CDF) followed the LAFD by accepting Incident Command System in 1980. That same year, the NWCW reviewed the ICS program; the members wanted to make certain ICS was truly the program California touted it to be.

Standing behind their product, the California State Marshall, the State Office of Emergency Services (OES), and the State

by Diana Sprain

Department of Forestry put their signatures on paper, all endorsing FIRESCOPE in 1981. A letter was sent to the National Wildfire Coordinating Group with the letters from the State officials. National Wildfire Coordinating Workgroup couldn't delay or push-off the recommendation. ICS was approved for national use. The US Forest Service started partial implementation in 1983 and completed department-wide use by 1985. ICS was so successful, versions of the system was adopted for use by law enforcement (LEICS). Even the medical community accepted a version of ICS (HEICS).

The adage, "those who fail to learn from the mistakes of the past are doomed to repeat them" is true in public safety. On 1 July, 1978, in Hackensack Ford, New Jersey, a fire claimed the lives of five firefighters. The roof collapsed one minute after the order to get out ('back out') was given by the Incident Commander (IC). Trapped firefighters managed to broadcast calls for help but no one caught those transmissions. The after action report noted that the order hadn't been acknowledged by dispatch or the Incident Commander, *but it had been heard by civilians listening to scanners.*

A few people monitoring their scanners actually called the fire dispatch when they heard the firefighters calling for help! In this incident, the field personnel were using only one channel. Fire grounds operations, EMS, personnel recalls, and regular dispatch operations were all working on a single frequency. The system was overwhelmed, one contributing reason that led to the deaths, as were the dispatchers overriding fire grounds traffic to put other radio transmissions.

Again, police and fire chiefs met at annual convention to discuss the safety of field personnel. How did one improve communications and keep the nation's law enforcement and firefighters safe at the same time? Training in street sense and fire ground awareness for field personnel, standardized policies & procedures, and better communications systems were cited, once more. It should be noted that one of the most important elements of the public safety system - the dispatchers - was overlooked. The personnel handling the radio, the Public Safety

What is Your Emergency? The History of Public Safety Dispatching in America

Telecommunicators, were ignored completely. Time and time again communications had been cited as an area of concern in after action reports. How many times would the Communications Center be pushed aside and left out in training sessions? Why weren't the personnel who manned the telephones, alarm boards, and radios considered important enough to be properly informed and trained?

It wasn't until the 1980's that the fire service came to understand the value of a trained dispatcher in a wildland fire incident thanks to agencies like San Jose (CA). San Jose trained their fire dispatchers in all aspects of the Incident Command System (ICS), but more importantly, they gave select personnel specialized fire ground training. Those Incident Management Team (IMT) dispatchers responded to the Incident Command Post for major fires to handle the radios, much like their counterparts, Tactical Dispatchers, did for SWAT incidents.

Fast forward seven years later. Another fire task force gave recommendations in December of 1987. This group was reporting on a follow-up to the famous report, "America Burning". This time, the group wrote: "The task force felt that resistance to change also occurs when society thrusts change and new responsibilities on the fire service. Further, society often requires that the fire service perform these additional tasks and functions without the accompanying resources and training…lack of standardization in communications and dispatching systems (can cause) problem for mutual or automatic aid; failure of the service management to become involved in national or regional fire service issues; and lack of professionalism at all levels of the fire service."

Dispatching finally received attention from the federal fire service in 2008. A United States Government task force under the authority of the United States Department of Agriculture and the Department of the Interior set a team of employees from multiple federal agencies to study current wildland fire dispatching. Consisting of members from the Bureau of Land Management, Department of the Interior, United States Forest Service, National Park Service, and the Fish & Wildlife Service, the team had their work cut out for them. The team released their findings as

by Diana Sprain

"Management Efficiency Assessment of the Interagency Wildland Fire Dispatch and Related Services" report. The intensive 184 page study concentrated specifically on the dispatch function at the *federal* wildland fire level. Anyone who had ever worked a wildland fire knew the list of agencies involved started with a local fire department then moving from city to county, to the state agencies, and finally to the federal responders. This was later identified in a follow-up study.

The Executive Committee pointed out four primary components of wildland fire dispatching: initial attack, resource coordination, expanded dispatch services for large incidents, and predictive services/intelligence gathering. The report noted:

- Each geographic area varies in vegetation/fuels, topography, weather, and climatology and fire potential conditions.
- Various types of disasters require unique responses.
- Agencies will continue to dispatch resources for wildland fire suppression.
- Dispatch must maintain interoperability across geographical areas.
- Standardization of dispatch personnel, equipment and operating procedures will be necessary to meet requirements.
- Dispatch and telecommunications technology is dynamic and continually evolving.

The team who did the study identified various areas for improvement, including operations and organization. Areas for dispatch were major points to be sure but the bigger picture was in management. In 2009, another federal group went over the 2008 report. This time, they also factored in law enforcement concerns. A pilot project, the Interagency Dispatch Improvement Project (IDIP) Steering Committee was established and two regional areas implemented pilot projects: one in California and another in the Southwest (Arizona, New Mexico, New Mexico, and west Texas). Sadly, even with updated dispatch systems, better technology, the

What is Your Emergency? The History of Public Safety Dispatching in America

National Incident Management System, and the Incident Command System (ICS), 19 firefighters lost their lives working a wildland fire in Yarnell, Arizona, on the 30th of June, 2013.

The National Fire Prevention Association (NFPA) is in charge of setting national standards for safety. Three sections: 1221, 1661, and 1710 reference Telecommunicators, Communications Centers, and radios. NFPA deals with Emergency Medical Dispatching in chapters four, five, and six. NFPA 1221 references standard for the installation, maintenance and use of communication systems for all three branches of Public Safety. NFPA 1710 has to do with response times to incidents.

"She's dead now. Thank you ma'am. Would you please send an ambulance?"

Up to the late 1960's old fashioned ambulances were rolling along status quo, with 50% of the companies run by mortuary companies or volunteers. In some cities, the ambulance was still rolling out of the local police station. Medical training of the personnel was a roll of the dice: if one was lucky if the attendants had general Red Cross first aid training. Chances were the dispatcher in the smaller companies was a relative of the company owner or a secretary. After hours, the phones may have rolled over to the owner, or stayed at the office, to be answered by the crew, if the company kept a 24 hour dispatch service.

We already learned this didn't change until a famous document was released in 1966 relating to Emergency Medical Services. The Committee on Trauma and Committee on Shock, from the Division of Medical Services of the National Academy of Sciences, a subdivision of the National Research Council published the land breaking report. This document, "Accidental Death and Disability: The National Disease of Modern Society" focused on injuries and deaths resulting from accidents. The report, also called 'The White Paper', was a critical look at the emergency medical system, from the time an accident occurred to the time the patient was admitted to the local emergency room. The Committee noted: "There is a need at the national level for the preparation of a manual delineating the available radio frequency channels, types and costs of equipment, and modifications of installation necessitated by local conditions. This is a function which should be the responsibility of the new National Highway Safety Agency in cooperation with the Federal Communications Commission, industry, and related groups. This agency is charged with the responsibility for establishing standards for all aspects of state highway safety programs, of which communications is an essential element."

The Committee made the following recommendations:

- Delineation of radio frequency channels and of equipment suitable to provide voice communication between ambulances, emergency departments, and other health-related agencies at community, regional, and national levels.
- Pilot studies across the nation for evaluation of models of radio and telephone installations to ensure effectiveness of communication facilities.
- Day-today use of voice communication facilities by the agencies serving emergency medical needs.
- Active exploration of the feasibility of designating a single nationwide telephone number to summon an ambulance.

The concepts were not new. Belfast, Ireland, had physicians riding in ambulances. England had a national 999 number in place in 1937 for its citizens to request help.

This report resulted in major revisions of standards of care for both field personnel and emergency rooms being established. Emergency Medical Technicians (EMT) and paramedic programs were developed across the country. Sadly, once again the dispatchers were left standing in the cold.

In Seattle, King County (WA), the famous Medic One emergency medical system was started to improve survival of cardiac arrest. The basics of the overall program include mandatory CPR training of High School students. Members of he

What is Your Emergency? The History of Public Safety Dispatching in America

pubic are encouraged to learn CPR as well. King County had the first Emergency Medical Dispatching program for its 911 dispatchers, which attracted the attention of Dr. Jeff Clawson when he was developing his own system.

Dr Clawson, a physician in Salt Lake City (UT), decided to take the recommendations one step further. There had been some attempts at 'medical instruction' programs, with fire departments staffing nurses or paramedics in dispatch. Dr. Clawson felt it was time for a radical change in public safety dispatching. The Emergency Medical Dispatch (EMD) program began by Dr. Jeff Clawson in 1977, another revolution in pre-hospital care. In his book, *Principles of Emergency Medical Dispatch*, Dr. Clawson stated: "In 1976, as the new, young contract medical advisor of the SLC (Salt Lake City) Fire Department, I promised to provide a medical dispatcher training course. But how? And what? EMT-type courses didn't seem appropriate because they were heavily treatment-orientated. More important, the priorities were lacking as they relate to medical dispatching. As a disciple of operating procedures for paramedic field activities, I felt that a protocol system could be the ticket. The fact that a dispatcher has limitations on time was well known. I first formulated the ideas for the Key Questions. Pre-arrival Instructions, and Dispatch Priorities…That the dispatcher is the first in the chain of response, but was the last to receive this attention, while unfortunate, has proven again the corollary that the 'last door opened often yields the greatest reward'". Dr. Clawson goes on to state, "With the recognition that the EMD is the 'first' first responder, however, the need to incorporate the activities of dispatch into the realm of medical control responsibility is obvious."

Having a protocol for pre-arrival instructional was necessary according to Dr. Clawson. Emergency Medical Services had already started upgrading the field personnel to an advanced level since the scathing White Paper was released in 1966. The next step was natural: get the emergency dispatchers trained. However, the resistance was strong in cities that offered medical advice by nurses or paramedics to screen calls, deciding whether ambulances were necessary or which way to send them (code two – no lights & sirens or code three – lights & sirens).

Dr. Clawson's thoughts on using nurses and/or paramedics came to light after a highly publicized event occurred in 1984. After the flames were put out, the details of the event shocked the nation. The incident itself primarily involved a nurse working for Dallas Fire Department. Soon agencies using nurses & paramedics to offer advice to callers reevaluated their procedures & policies.

The call for help started just as other request for an ambulance did: with a telephone call made to 911. Larry Boeff asked for an ambulance on behalf of his stepmother when she complained of trouble breathing. The call was answered by a dispatcher, who for an unknown reason was unable to determine a clear cut complaint. Per the department procedure at the time, the dispatcher transferred Mr. Boeff to a nurse. That nurse, Billie Myrick, demanded to speak to Larry's stepmother. Obviously upset, Mr. Boeff told the nurse his mother couldn't get to the phone because of her condition. He went on to repeatedly tell Ms. Myrick, as response to her further questions, his mother was incoherent.

Mr. Boeff's answers were laced with four letter words, no doubt a result of his stress relating to his mother's medical condition. Public Safety Dispatchers deal with angry, upset, distressed callers every day who use foul language during their conversations. The majority of the time, the colorful language isn't directed at the dispatcher personally, it's more about the situation. In the Boeff call, Myrick decided she didn't want to listen to the caller's 'verbal abuse' any longer. Nurse Myrick hadn't learned how to disconnect herself from the caller's situational language and get to the point of the call. Instead, she connected Mr. Boeff with Dallas Police Captain Greene, who told him to cooperate and put his mother on the phone. Another round of explanations about his mother's condition ended with Mr. Boeff speaking to Myrick again; resulting in the frustrated Boeff hanging up – without an ambulance being sent. He did call back, starting out again with Nurse Myrick demanding to speak to his mother, but this time he angrily tells the Dallas nurse, "She is dead now. Thank you ma'am.

What is Your Emergency? The History of Public Safety Dispatching in America

Would you please send an ambulance? Would you please send an ambulance here?"

Eight minutes from the time Larry Boeff made his first phone call to 911, an ambulance arrives on scene to find the woman unresponsive. The death of the patient ignited a media firestorm, not just in Dallas, but nationwide. Why, the media reported, didn't Dallas Fire just send an ambulance when any person with half a brain could tell the mother was ill by her son's description? As a nurse, shouldn't Ms. Myrick have known what difficulty breathing or incoherent meant? Even when the nurse had missed the boat, why didn't the Police Captain figure it out and what of the initial dispatcher? Weren't there any standing protocols in place? Remember, Salt Lake City Fire Department already had their Emergency Medical Dispatching system established. From the moment the 911 call placed by the Boeff family was answered until the time the Dallas Fire Department finally dispatched the emergency medical services, every action was a tragedy of errors. This was truly an unfortunate incident, and one every dispatcher should be learn about, if nothing else, but for preventative sake.

Chapter Five: 9-1-1: I Know Where You Are

While I was training as a Public Safety Dispatcher I was nervous about taking my first 911 call. I had reviewed *how* to interview a caller, what to ask, how to guide the person to get the information I needed, and so on. I had listened to my trainer answer the phones and marveled at how smoothly she handled the various requests. When the big day came, I was almost shaking.

Wouldn't you know that very FIRST call was a silent hold-up alarm at a bank? Per protocol, I made the call to the institution and the employee confirmed that the bank had just been held up. I managed to calm the teller down and get descriptions of the suspects. Next call? No problem!

Operator, I Need Help!

"One ringy-dingy, two ringy-dingy" with her eyes squinting Lily Tomlin gracefully answered phones, plugging in to one line then another. Her comedic genius as Ernestine, the nosy telephone operator had us in tears as she interfered, interjected, and just plain caused havoc as she put in her two cents in her customer's lives. More often than not, Ernestine hung up on her customers.

As much as we laughed at Ernestine's antics, the real Ma Bell operators were a lifeline for millions of frightened people before 9-1-1 was even an idea. Going back beyond the telephone for a bit how did one request assistance in an emergency? The easiest method was to send someone to the source. Help arrived, hopefully before the patient passed away, the house burned, or the criminal exited stage left. People were self-sufficient back then and handled most of their problems by themselves or perhaps with assistance of their neighbors. Country doctors handled a wide range of medical problems while the local law enforcement knew residents by first name. Cops were familiar with their townsfolk's routines. People were suspicious of strangers and generous with neighbors. News was passed along via newspapers, newsletters, or word of mouth (town's criers). Instead of a Hue & Cry, in times of need, a Sheriff would ask for volunteers for a posse.

What is Your Emergency? The History of Public Safety Dispatching in America

    The phone company's operators (the 'o' number) were doing a good job taking emergency calls and transferring the callers to the local police, fire, or ambulance agencies, but the public safety community agreed the system needed an overall improvement. Bell Telephone was averaging over 40,000 calls a day for emergency service, and that was via the Operator. How many calls for service were coming in to the police or fire communications centers via transfer from a desk sergeant or alarm board? How much time could be shaved off, how many lives saved, if the public could dial a quick & simple emergency number to reach the appropriate agency right away? Consider Los Angeles County in the 1970's, with 50 different law enforcement agencies. Trying to remember the phone numbers for the various departments was tough enough for other agencies, and darn near impossible for residents. In those days, local agencies went around handing out round stickers with the seven-digit telephone numbers to their department to residents and businesses. The decals were placed on the phone itself. Ambulance services did the same, handing out 'free' merchandise consisting of paper pads, pens, and stickers with their company logo and telephone number. In a crunch, which number did you call in an emergency? The one on your phone dial or the one printed on the pad of paper.

    Remember how reports such as the White Paper opened up the eyes of Public Safety agencies across the country to the terrible response to accidents and trauma? Study after study came to the same conclusion. A nationwide single source number was needed for the public to access emergency help. Realizing something needed to be done to improve emergency medical response cities like Philadelphia, Pittsburgh, Los Angeles, and Miami started pilot paramedic programs. Most people were familiar with Los Angeles County Fire Department's paramedic service due to the 1970's television show, *Emergency!* Meanwhile the President's Commission on Law Enforcement and Administration of Justice released a document called "The Challenge of Crime in a Free Society" in February of 1967. This report was to law enforcement what the White Paper was to Emergency Medical Services, with an extensive look at every aspect of crime in America. When it came to calling the police for help, the Commission noted: "In trying to call the police from an ordinary telephone, a person may be bewildered by the many police jurisdictions and the various telephone numbers associated with them. In Los Angeles area alone, there are there are 50 different telephone numbers that reach police departments within Los Angeles County. It should be possible to have a single telephone number to reach the police directly. England has such a universal number."

In 1972, another Presidential Commission was charged with reviewing fire safety by President Nixon. After completing an in-depth study, the National Commission of Fire Prevention and Control released their report, entitled "America Burning" on May 4, 1973. One of the recommendations by the Commission was for agencies to pool their resources and have regional communications centers, instead of individual dispatch centers, to improve response times of firefighting units. The Commission acknowledged that fire departments were taking more responsibility for medical and rescue calls, but the concern was aired over the fire personnel not having training for said calls. According to the results gathered by the Commission, "…or they are requiring firefighters to handle some patients they are not trained to handle. Or they are compiling a poor record of response to non-fire emergencies because they have an inadequate communication and deployment systems."

The idea of a simple, nationwide number to call for help was already in use in Europe. England developed the 999 number, placing the emergency number in service on July 8, 1937. Winnipeg, Manitoba added the 999 service in 1959, but later changed the emergency number to 911 to match that of the United States. The United Kingdom was known for its advances in emergency care. Belfast, Ireland had the first advanced pre-hospital care ambulances. Europe, proper, handled EMS a little differently, sending physicians in ambulances instead of paramedical personnel.

American Telegraph & Telephone (AT&T) and the Federal Communications Commission (FCC) had discussed the possibility of a similar system in the United States in the mid 60's. The Association of Public Safety Communications Officers (later

What is Your Emergency? The History of Public Safety Dispatching in America

changed to Officials), or APCO, started pressuring the FCC and the phone company to adopt the concept of a nationally-recognized and dedicated emergency number. In 1967, the FCC and AT & T sat down to hash out the details of the emergency number.

A municipality-controlled emergency number would be financially beneficial to the phone company. With emergency calls handled by police or fire departments, instead of phone company operators, Bell Company (AT & T) could potentially reduce staffing costs. The big question in the phone company's mind was the logistics of call routing and jurisdictional boundaries.

When the actual digits were selected, AT & T already had certain rules about area codes. Long distance area codes had a zero or a one as the second digit whereas any other number combination was a local call; the telephone switching station recognized 911 as a special number (the same as it did 211, 411, and 611). 911 had yet to be assigned by the phone company to any other use. AT & T's work towards designing the emergency number would only affect the Bell Companies, not any other independent phone companies as AT & T had no authority over those businesses.

According to an article by Alan Burton, "The U.S. Independent Telephone Association was certainly not pleased that AT&T had plunged ahead with this plan that would affect them too. The Association circulated a letter stating, "In most of our communities there is no such organization as a single public safety agency. It may therefore be a problem to form such an agency and provide the funds necessary for the rental of switchboards and other necessary telephone equipment. There may be differences of opinion as to who should operate such an agency because of jurisdictional conflicts between state police, sheriffs and local police. In addition there will be the responsibility of handling fire calls and ambulance calls, perhaps from volunteer organizations which are not tied in with the police. In a report dated February 27, 1968, FCC Commissioner Lee Loevinger wrote, "It appears ... that there are these objections to the plan: (A) The Bell System [meaning AT&T] did not consult with the various police organizations, independent [telephone] companies, and others about this specific proposal prior to its announcement."

by Diana Sprain

Indiana Representative J Edward Roush (D) was foremost in pushing legislation through Congress to get the emergency 911 declaration approved. Bell Phone Systems had to establish a policy to absorb the cost of central office modifications & additions to get the 911 code as part of the base rate. The phone subscriber would pay for the 911 service according to tarifed rates and those taxes would help pay for the equipment. With Representative Roush's efforts, Congress passed the legislation setting the numbers 9-1-1 aside for a national emergency number. Representative Roush made the announcement at a Washington DC press conference. The next question was who would get the first 911 system?

On 8th November, 1967, House Congressional Resolution 361 was adopted, stating that "The United States should have one uniform nationwide fire reporting telephone number and one uniform nationwide police reporting telephone number." In addition, the document discussed regionalized dispatch centers, coinless dialing ability for emergency calls, and the actual number to be used for the single emergency number.

Alabama Telephone Company president Bob Gallagher aggressively fought to get the new 911 system in his state. On January 15, 1968, he read aloud an article in the Wall Street Journal on the new emergency number. Bob, and Inside State Plant Manager Robert Fitzgerald, decided on Haleyville for the first installation site. Robert selected his technical team: Jimmy White, Glenn Johnston, Al Bush, and Pete Gosa. The phone company worked diligently towards the startup date of February 16, 1968. The hard work paid off, and on February 16th, Alabama Speaker of the House Rankin Fite made the first 911 call to the Haleyville Police Department, answered by Representative Tom Beville, with the city Mayor James Whitt, Bob Gallagher, and Alabama Public Service Commissioner Eugene Connor observing. The era of 9-1-1 had officially begun. The red-colored telephone they used to make that call is now in the Haleyville Museum.

The White House's Office of Telecommunications issued a national policy statement in March of 1973 recognizing the importance and benefits of the new 911 number. The White House encouraged the nation-wide adoption of 911. A Federal

What is Your Emergency? The History of Public Safety Dispatching in America

Information Center was founded to help governmental agencies start their own 911 programs.

Bottom line: the Federal Government recommended 911 but couldn't mandate the new emergency number. Even today (2016), there are few areas in the US without 911 services or only offering basic or enhanced 911. The Next Genergation 911 (NG911) is yers away due to logistics of internet and and telecomunications equipment availability in rural and remote locations.

I know what number you are calling from.

The new emergency 9-1-1 service didn't catch on right away. Even in the mid 1970's there were large metropolitan cities without the 911 service. Agencies were leery of the new technology while others needed funding assistance to get the equipment & system in place. Dispatchers needed training in the use of the system. Convincing the public a new tax was necessary to pay for the service *in case* they might need to use the system wasn't an easy sell.

For cities and counties without 9-1-1, the public continued to rely on the standard seven digit emergency number or dialing '0' for the operator. In major metropolitan areas this could be problematic. For example, Los Angeles County is made up of many smaller cities, along with the City of Las Angeles and the patchwork sections of Los Angeles County territory. In parts of the County, there are literally four jurisdictions which come together at an intersection. Until the cities & county signed automatic mutual response agreements, a caller could get very frustrated trying to get a police unit to come out for a non-injury accident.

911 did have some unintended consequences. For agencies that put 911 in place, the call volume increased substantially. Before 911, people only called the cops when absolutely necessary. Speculation was that citizens either didn't know the local number or didn't want to go through the operator. Once 911 was in place, the residents felt empowered to use the service. Not only did they public call the police for their perceived complaint, they expected a response. Patrolman spent less time doing 'routine'

by Diana Sprain

patrol. Dispatchers were taking more requests for service. Was this good or bad? Had the crime rates suddenly increased due to a crime spree or was the availability of the system to report crime the reason for the increased statistics?

The first 911 version released was the Basic 911. The developers decided to name dispatch centers which received the 911 calls, Public Safety Answering Points or, PSAPS. Primary PSAPS were generally assigned to law enforcement call centers. For agencies that split responsibilities of fire & law enforcement dispatching between two different buildings, a secondary PSAP was set-up to allow 911 call transfers from law enforcement to the fire dispatchers. In some larger areas, 911 calls for ambulances required another transfer. How does a 911 work? In simplest terms, when the three digit 911 number is dialed, the call is routed via a telephone trunk line from the local phone at the telephone company and then sent via a switch to the appropriate PSAP, or sent directly to the PSAP. This system was set-up to work on hard-lined phones (regular house or business lines). When the phone was answered at the PSAP, the area code and phone number displayed the Automated Number Identification (ANI). The downside to Basic 911 was not having a location. In cases of hang-ups or callers too incapacitated to speak, dispatch personnel had to call the phone company security service to get a location of the phone number – which was the billing address. That took time, which wasted precious minutes in a true emergency.

Training the residents and businesses in the communities which embraced 911 was another chore. Agencies had to send out personnel to community meetings to educate residents and businesses on when and how to use 911. Departments had to decide on 911 hang-up call policies: would a full component of equipment get dispatched or just a patrol unit: or, would dispatch make the attempt to call the number back first? What about harassing calls to the communications centers (kids dialing 911, drunks, non-emergency calls)? Some states went as far as to adopt criminal codes relating to the misuse of 911.

The next level of 911 released was the Enhanced 911. Enhanced 911 combined the basic phone number to a data base

What is Your Emergency? The History of Public Safety Dispatching in America

maintained by the phone company of addresses. This listing is called a Master Street Address Guide (MSAG). The early 1970's started with a trial basis of the E911 program in Alameda County, California. This 'selective call routing' feature took a lot of guess work from the call-taking aspect of dispatching. Locations of occurrences still needed to be verified, but at least a dispatcher had a starting point for a 911 hang-up.

This updated version displayed the ANI and the Automated Location Identification (ALI). With the new Enhanced 911 the phone number and location displayed on a screen when the call was answered in the Public Safety Answering Point. That was a game changer for Public Safety personnel. Residential addresses showed apartment numbers, businesses showed names and suite numbers. What Enhanced 911 didn't display was a specific location in a large business using a PBX service. For example, a dispatcher getting a 911 call from an employee at a multi-storey building, such as a hotel or hospital, reporting a fight would only see the main address, not which floor or unit the employee was located. It was up to the dispatcher to get the actual physical location from the employee. Still, having a location was 100% better than nothing and 50% better than just a phone number.

Were there flaws in the system? Yes, as with any technology bugs exist. For example, one evening our PSAP received a 911 call from a woman requesting an ambulance. She called from a payphone and the dispatcher answering the call verified the address. Fire and ems went out but couldn't find her. The call was cancelled as 'gone on arrival'. A second call was received from the hysterical woman asking where the ambulance was. Again, the payphone showed her in our city but she was no where to be found. A quick thinking dispatcher kept her on the phone this time and asked if she saw the responders. When she answered no, we became suspicious and asked her *what city* she was in. Turns out, she was in the neighboring city. The street and numerics were the same as the locaiton in ours. We contacted that city and requested the services be dispatched and filled out a form to the phone company requesting a change to the 911 routing for that particular payphone.

It was estimated that roughly 17% of the US population could call 911 by the end of 1976. The number served by 911 jumped to 26% at the end of 1979. In 1987, half of the US population had access to 911.

911 changed again when cellular phones hit the market. Wireless Phase 1 was mandated in 2000 by the Federal Communications Commission, requiring mobile cell phone companies to transmit the location of the nearest receiving antenna (cell site). Phase II required the cellular carriers to enable phones to transmit the location of wireless phone callers within 300 meters via latitude & longitude coordinates. Crying about the costs, many cellular vendors asked for waivers. Meanwhile, mobile phone calls were routed to State Police or Highway Patrol – inundating those PSAPs with requests for assistance meant for local city or sheriff departments. Unlike the traditional phones, cellular callers had to be able to verbalize a location of their emergency. That was difficult in rural areas with little or no reference points for travelers. Older phones didn't have the GPS chips which came with the newer models.

By 2005, Phase II was still in the implementation mode. The Federal Communications Commission required phones either send location via GPS coordinates (longitude & latitude) or by triangulation from cell sites. This did not release the Public Safety Telecommunicator from verifying the caller's location.

What is your non-emergency? 3-1-1 is open for business

October 2, 1996 was the first day the public in Baltimore (MD) had a choice: 911 for emergencies or 311 for non-emergencies. The reason given for implementing a new three digit non-emergency number was to provide relief to the overburdened Public Safety Answering Point. Residents of Baltimore were calling 911 for all incidents, not having access to a regular non-emergency number. After the non-emergency number's establishment, the 911 system experienced a drop in calls, thanks to the new 311 system. But, was it a blessing or a burden?

What is Your Emergency? The History of Public Safety Dispatching in America

311 had great potential and a few flaws. Unlike the 911 system, the 311 didn't come with an Automated Number Identification (ALI) or Automated Location Identification (ANI): all calls were received in the 'blind', or anonymous. The hardware was pricy. How would 311 calls be documented? Would the 311 calls be entered in the Computer-Aided Dispatch (CAD) system or just logged on a spread sheet? Who would handle the responses? In many cases, 311 calls didn't require Public Safety unit, instead animal control, public works, or another city division could take care of the incident instead of a police officer or fire company. On the upside, the burden of the 'nuisance' calls flooding communications centers could be redirected to another call-taking center allowing 911 Public Safety Answering Points to concentrate on emergency incidents.

The non-emergency 311 was slow to be accepted by the public safety professionals. They had a reasonable excuse: what if the citizens mistook 311 for 911? A citizen calling 311 for a burglary in progress instead of 911 could be a huge mistake. Would a non-trained 311 operator recognize an emergency in time and transfer the reporting party to 911? The Association for Public Safety Communications Officials, Inc. (APCO) and the National Emergency Number Association (NENA) expressed concerns and gave recommendations. President Bill Clinton endorsed the new number as part of his 1996 campaign. The Federal Communications Commission approved the new national 311 number on February 19, 1997.

Even after 311 had been approved by the government, it wasn't accepted as quickly as expected. Some major cities: Las Vegas (NV), Detroit (MI), San Jose (CA), and New York (NY) adopted the 311 service. Not every agency assigned 311 to the local law enforcement Public Safety Answering Point, the reasoning being that their dispatchers were already busy enough. In those cases, 311 was allotted to Public Works or out-sourced to an independent call center altogether. In *Managing Calls to the Police with 911/311 Systems* Mazerole & Rogan stated:

"Introduction of 311 in Baltimore fundamentally changed how citizens reported certain crime and disorder incidents to 911.

For example, before 311, police received about 700 calls per week regarding family disturbances. After 311, family disturbance calls to 911 declined by about 200 per week. Citizen calls to 911 of juvenile disturbances, parking violations, suspicious persons, and destruction of property also declined. More intriguing is the 87 percent decline in citizen loud noise complaints to 911 even though total number of loud noise complaints increased – most of those placed to 311. Many citizen reports for narcotics, motor vehicle theft, gambling, larceny, and aggravated assault migrated from 911 to 311, and the overall volume of calls in some of those categories also increased. The researchers speculate that 311 call anonymity may be factor in call volume increases."

You can't find me: 911 Abuse

After the establishment of 911 for quick access to emergency help, a new problem raised its ugly head: the 911 abuser. Public Safety Answering Points (PSAPs) began receiving calls from people who had nothing better to do or who were angry at the police for various reasons. PSAPs across the United States recorded an incredible amount of harassing phone calls on the 911 lines, in some cases, triple digit numbers over a very short period.

These incidents were classified as annoyances at first, and in many instances the individual agencies were helpless to do much other than file harassment charges against the perpetrators. In one case, a suspect called an agency's 911 line constantly from Friday night through Monday morning, to the point that it literally had one dispatcher dedicated to him (and a 911 line as well). After a bit of creative investigation and transferring of calls, the subject was positively identified and charges filed with the Public Safety Answering Point as the 'victim'. The suspect was tried, convicted, and spent six months in the county jail for his crime against 911. Alas, that successful ending is not as common as agencies would like. The department did have a recording dispatchers could transfer abusers to, with the message stating that misdialing 911 for harassment was a crime.

What is Your Emergency? The History of Public Safety Dispatching in America

911 callers upped the ante when cell phones came out. Unlike the legacy or payphones, cellular phones created an entirely new set of problems. Any phone was required to have the ability to dial 911 provided it had a charged battery. A pre-paid cell phone was released to the public that didn't require any product registration, contract, or even a name or address of the user. In a press release dated 29th of April, 2002, the Federal Communications Commission wrote: "Non-initialized wireless telephones are phones that are not registered for service with any Commercial Mobile Radio Service (CMRS) carrier. Because carriers generally assign a dialable number to a handset only when a customer enters into a service contract, a non-initialized phone lacks a dialable telephone number. Examples of these types of phones include "911-only" phones as well as unsubscribed cellular phones distributed by donation programs to at-need individuals, such as victims of domestic violence."

Voice over Internet Protocol (VoIP) phones added another dimension. People kept their numbers and service when they moved from area to another. It was difficult to know where the caller physically was unless queried by the dispatcher. Invariably, a dispatch center received a 911 call from a caller in another state. Another notable incident occurred when one caller dialed 911 from a military base in another country using a VoIP phone registered to an address in the continental USA. The dispatcher had to make numerous calls before determining where the incident was happening. Once she found the location, she was able to contact the military and request the military police respond.

Even cellular phones can be problematic if the public uses older models not set up with GPS devices or in remote areas with minimal coverage. It puts a burden upon a dispatcher to help a reporting party with an emergency completely potentially out of their jurisdiction. There is some help for the Communications Centers: the Federal Communications Commission maintains a data base of registered 911 Public Safety Answering Points (PSAPs). This information is available for official use by communications center personnel.

by Diana Sprain

Cellular callers discovered they were able to dial 911 and bother the communications center personnel with ease. Many of the abusers used throw-away phones, the pay-for-use devices not requiring any registration before the phone would work. Even disconnected cellular phones will still dial 911 providing the battery is charged per government regulation. This added to another type of problem. A phenomenon referred to as "Swatting" was the next step in the 911 harassment. The trouble usually starts with a notification to a Public Safety Answering Point. The caller reports an in-progress crime, generally involving a SWAT-type situation (kidnapping, barricaded subject, hostage, domestic violence) at a residence. The information may be 'second-hand' via a Facebook (or other social media) post or while the current reporting party is supposedly having a conversation with the resident. The police dispatcher takes the information in good faith, and field personnel are dispatched. Once everyone arrives, they discovered the call is false. The reporting person, phone numbers, and names given are phony. In many cases, the incident locations are at homes of celebrities.

Finally, the latest crime against Public Safety Answering Points is the Telephony Denial of Service, or TDoS. In this case, a Public Safety Answering Point is contacted by a perpetrator representing a phony collections company. The representative asks to speak with a former or current employee about a debt. When denied (as most agencies have policies regarding employees handling personal business on company time), the caller refuses to relinquish the line and gets aggressive with demanding the money owed, threatening to keep calling back.

In a number of cases, the phony company launches a TDoS attack, tying up incoming and outgoing lines to the point that the department has to switch to an alternate call center. This is a federal crime: agencies targeted are urged to document all details, refuse to pay the ransom money, and contact the FBI as soon as possible

Some states have had laws enacted, making false calls to 911 a misdemeanor crime, with penalties depending on the circumstances. Some states also gave dispatchers the same immunities that field personnel enjoyed (provided they stayed within their agency's policies & procedures).

Huzzah for the red phone!!

Haleyville, Alabama is known for more than just being the scene of the first 911 telephone call. The city is the center of an annual 911 Festival each year. The idea came from Haleyville Mayor Ray Boshell. The first 911 festival was held in 1994; and every year since. First Responders are honored with a parade, booths with information, and games. The local law enforcement, fire, emergency medical services, and emergency room personnel get involved, along with surrounding agencies. Haleyville posts photographs of the events on its website and invites all interested folks to come and check it out.

President George Bush signed the first proclamation declaring the week of April 14-20, National Public Safety Telecommunicators Week in 1992. Subsequent proclamations were signed in 1994 and 1996 by President Bill Clinton. The idea for a week honoring our Nation's dispatchers began in Contra Costa County, California. Patricia Anderson of the Contra Costa Sheriff's Department got the ball rolling in 1981. She called it National Dispatcher's Week. Three years later, the concept was taken up by APCO Chapters in Virginia and North Carolina. They made certain the resolution was placed on APCO's agenda. Congressional Representative Edward J. Markey (D) of Massachusetts signed on to the cause, introducing H.J Resolution 284 to Congress. By then, in California, many agencies were putting on their own Telecommunicator weeks, official or not.

In the mid 1990's, after multiple attempts, Congress finally accepted the resolution. The week is now officially known as the Public Safety Telecommunicators Week. Instead of just honoring dispatchers, it also thanks the radio technicians and folks that support telecommunications. Across the country, agencies honor their Public Safety Telecommunicators (Dispatchers) for a job well done and it's all thanks to Patricia Anderson.

Is the 911 system perfect? No, there will always be flaws in any technology but it beats having no service or going back to the old fashioned dialing '0' for help.

Chapter Six: Public Safety Dispatchers as a Profession

"Fill up your gas tank, 'cause you're gonna see the city."

The smart field personnel, no matter whether they are law enforcement, fire, or EMS, learn to respect dispatchers early in their careers. A good dispatcher can have a field unit going from call to call without a break in the action from the moment the unit goes in service until the last minute of the shift; and, he will make it look legitimate. I learned that lesson from an old style dispatcher. "Joe" would treat EMTs and medics according to how they took care of him (bring him food, drinks, run the occasional errand, take that transfer call without a complaint, etc.). Complain about a run, whine about bringing him a sandwich (from the 'free' food fridge at a local hospital) and Joe would make it his goal for the day to have you spend the rest of the shift handling non-emergency transfer calls back-to-back instead of running emergencies. The smart ones shut up while foolish ones who complained to a supervisor would spend their next shift running non-emergency calls as well. Usually they clued in pretty quick and apologized with an appropriate 'gift'.

Times have changed. What was once called education, jokes, or hazing has now become 'bullying'. One has to be careful in his or her actions. Joe's treatment of dispatchers – or emergency medical personnel - would never be tolerated today.

How does any person become a Public Safety Telecommunicator, or Dispatcher? We've discovered the early dispatchers transferred from other divisions. Many were phone operators or secretaries. Department heads & chiefs kept their eyes open for likely candidates, encouraging those people to apply, or come in for an interview.

As times progressed, so did the hiring process. Emergency Medical Services agencies continued the minimal steps of accepting applications, selecting those they wished to interview and picking the candidate they felt was the best person. Whether the dispatcher had a background in emergency medical services varied according to the company. In some departments, being a

by Diana Sprain

certified Emergency Medical Technician or paramedic was a requirement in order to provide some pre-arrival instructions.

Before the fire department joined the EMS transportation game, the private ambulances handled patient transports in many areas. In large cities like Los Angeles (CA) and San Francisco (CA) it was a mixture of privates and the fire or health department which dealt with ambulance calls. Eventually, San Francisco Health Department turned over the EMS business to the Fire Department. The battle was not only to get the 911 responder contract, but to lock-up the non-emergency transport contracts as well. Some counties issued a guarantee of payment (a minimal fee) in case the patient was unable to pay, or to help cover costs in the event of a cancellation. Competition for the contracts was fierce, as mocked by the movie *Mother, Juggs, & Speed.*

As calls came in to dispatch, it was not unusual to give a standard eta of 10-15 minutes to the fire or police dispatcher, even if there were no units actually available! After hanging up, the dispatcher would start calling units, pushing them to clear hospitals as quickly as possible. In one case, a company I worked for sent out dispatch personnel in plain clothes while a supervisor covered the communications center. The company in question required its dispatchers to be certified Emergency Medical Technicians for just that reason. What is funny is how the 'back-up' crew was dressed: men in slacks, jacket & tie and women in dresses or skirt & blouse. Why the business attire? The ambulance division was run by its parent company: a mortuary service. The dispatchers handled front counter duties, hence the reason for a dress code. They certainly turned a few heads on scene and at the hospital. Once the call was complete, they drove back to dispatch and went back to handling radio calls and the phones as if nothing had happened.

In the seventies, many of the smaller ambulances were using desk-top radios. A secondary purpose for emergency medical service radios is to connect to hospitals in order to provide communications. The Hospital Emergency and Administrative Radio (HEAR) program came about in the 1960's in response to the release of the White Paper. Field units could call a report about a patients' condition to a hospital emergency room. The original

What is Your Emergency? The History of Public Safety Dispatching in America

HEAR radios worked with two radio frequencies: a local channel 155.340 to talk to local hospitals and a regional channel 155.280 for hospitals to speak to each other. Now, the regional channel is considered a nationwide network.

Jumping Through the Hoops

How does one become a Public Safety Dispatcher? Perspective Telecommunicators can contact their local 911 Public Safety Answering point and check to see if the center allows 'sit-alongs'. Spending a couple of hours is a good method of determining if the profession is the right fit for the individual. Some agencies will allow the potential applicant to fill out an interest card. When the agency opens up the applications for a specified position, the department will send out a card or email with the notification. Other places to look for open dispatcher positions can be with different local, state, or federal agency websites. Your state's Peace Officers Standards & Training (POST) office may have a list of dispatching classes in your area.

Recruiting personnel for a Public Safety Telecommunications job is no easy task. Whether a department is a small city, a medium-sized county, or a state agency, the basic job of a dispatcher is the same: gather information, determine a course of action, and dispatch field units to handle the incident. Of course, *how* one obtains the information varies from agency to agency. Each department may use a different *method* of sorting data and determining what to do with the resulting information. No two agencies are alike in regards to policies and procedures. Radio codes, Computer-Aided Dispatch (CAD) systems, jurisdictions, the amount of field units, police only, fire only, combined police/fire, single dispatcher verses multiple dispatcher, or primary verses secondary PSAP all play a part in the dispatcher's job. Once the Telecommunicator has decided how to handle a call, he/she must dispatch units but even that seemingly simple task is not always so easy. Small departments may have limited resources after certain hours which require paging out personnel while other agencies may only allow off-duty recalls in specific situations due to budget restrictions.

First step in the recruitment process is getting out the word that an agency or company is accepting applications. Before personal computers and the Internet were invented, people found jobs the old-fashioned way: perusing the help wanted ads in the newspaper, via job fairs, recommendations from family and/or co-workers, and by referrals from the unemployment office. Over the years, public safety's application for dispatchers grew from a simple form to the detailed paperwork most agencies require today. There was a time when a person's word was good enough to land them a job, but sadly, that's no longer true.

Once you have found an agency that is accepting applications, one must meet the basic qualifications for the job. *Entry* level applications are for persons with no prior experience. *Lateral* jobs are for persons with experience. For example, the State of Nevada has five levels of Public Safety Dispatchers (PSDs). The first is PSD I, which is the entry level job. PSD II and III are experienced dispatchers with different amounts of job experience & time in service. A PSD IV is a supervisor and the PSD V is a manager/director. I currently work for the Nevada Department of Wildlife. We have one dispatch center for the entire state compared to the Department of Public Safety (Highway Patrol) which has three regional centers. Some of the sheriff departments have a primary and one or two secondary dispatch centers. The larger cities may only have one center but they split their jurisdiction into radio zones with each channel assigned to a different dispatcher.

Find a department that is looking for the level of training and job experience you have. A jumpstart to getting a job in telecommunications can be done by taking a Public Safety Dispatcher class at your local community college. Time as a Police Explorer is useful. College degrees are not required but it never hurts. Get a scanner and listen to radio traffic for the department you are interested in. Learn about the agency via books or their website. Be honest when filling out the application documents.

What is Your Emergency? The History of Public Safety Dispatching in America

Lies will come back to haunt you later and can disqualify the applicant from being considered.

The hiring process varies according to the specific area of public safety the dispatcher candidate chooses. If the dispatcher candidate passes the initial paper screening by the Human Resources, then the next step will most likely be a written test. In the case of a dispatcher already working at a different agency, the written test may be waved depending upon experience. Applicants should check with the hiring agency's Human Resources on this.

Some regions combine costs and sponsor a test, with the names of those who pass given out to each department. One can no longer buy a generic "Arco' Civil service exam book and expect to pass a Public Safety Telecommunicator test. The components of the exam might consist of a series of alpha-numeric strings of characters read out loud for the test takers to write down, starting out slow and gradually getting faster; a quick scenario played on a video screen of which the audience must then write down answers to questions; grammar; spelling; simple mapping; and decision making skills.

There was a time when few departments performed a practical test. That has changed. Many dispatch supply companies offer simulator devices for practical training and testing. Dispatcher candidates may encounter such a device during the hiring process. The next step is often an interview.

Interviews are a critical component of the hiring process. Law enforcement and fire departments generally have a handful of personnel sit in a room and ask candidates a predetermined set of questions. This called an oral board. It may be intimidating, but all public safety personnel will most likely face an oral board at some point in their career. Panel members can be from the hiring agency or outside departments and may be a mix of sworn or civilian personnel. Depending on the number of candidates being interviewed, each member of the panel may ask a specific question, or one designated person will do the interview while the others mostly take notes and only jump in if they have wish to clarify one of your responses.

Here it is true you only get one chance to make a good impression. Be clean, dressed up, well rested, and have a good breakfast. The day before, drive to the destination, find where to park, the building where the interview will be held, and the room number. Be ready and confident.

Greet the oral board members as they are introduced, shake their hands and only then should the dispatcher candidate sit down. After the interview, thank each member for their time. A candidate may chose to bring a resume to the interview and offer to leave a copy with the members. Some may say this is incorrect, but everywhere I have done this I walked out with empty hands and a callback later. Interviewees should be honest, to the point, and look the person asking the question direct in the eye when answering. You will be asked about why you want the position and any relevant job history. The board may ask what you would do in some basic (generic) situations. Be realistic when answering: you aren't expected to know the department's polices & procedures.

Here's where the process starts to vary quite a bit. Most law enforcement agencies perform a State and Federal fingerprint-based background check on perspective dispatch employees due to Department of Justice mandates. Public Safety Telecommunicators have access to sensitive information, criminal history, and limited personnel records. How far and deep the agency performing the rest of the background goes is up to the individual department, including up to the same investigation process performed as is done on law enforcement officers – which may include a polygraph and/or drug screen tests. Other options on the pre-employment red-tape can be medical exams, hearing tests, and psychological interview. One of my medical exams included a doctor standing across a room whispering. I had to repeat what he said – it was my 'hearing' test. Another agency sent me to an actual audiology lab for a formal hearing exam. It all comes down to money.

If you manage to get through everything, you may receive a written offer of employment or be placed on a hiring list. With a job acceptance, the next step is the official start date. If the position requires you to re-locate, time consideration on the start date will be negotiable.

What Was I Thinking? Learning to do the job

Training of the Public Safety Telecommunicator can be a whirlwind affair or a long, drawn out process. As it was decades ago in many agencies, today's training can be an on-the-job experience or a formal classroom affair. Many dispatchers still walk in to the Communications Center, are handed a headset, a pad of paper and maybe a few handouts and told "You'll figure out most of this as time goes on."

When I took a Pubic Safety Dispatcher position at one agency, I was assigned to train with a senior officer. After three days he looked at me and said "I'm outta here: you know what you're doing." He left me alone. Sure, I knew how to use a radio but I didn't know any of the policies or procedures. I had to figure out things on my own. Later, when the agency decided to use the computer-aided dispatch system available as part of the records management system (but had never used), I self-taught myself how to use the program by reading the help files. I was then designated the department trainer and given eight (yes, that's right, eight) hours to train a handful of trainers who would go on to teach the rest of the staff on their shifts how to work the software.

One dispatcher learning his or her duties via the 'on-the-job' training method is not the most efficient manner of training. The best way is via a formal dispatch academy, similar to the law enforcement officers or firefighters. No department in their right mind would release an officer or firefighter to the job with only a manual of policies and procedures to 'learn the job'. Why is it acceptable for dispatchers to learn as they go? Trainees should have special room with access to a simulator, a training section of the computer-aided dispatcher program (CAD), and practice with radios. One agency I visited had a great training room that allowed trainers and trainees to listen to live radio traffic and log in the the CAD system (training or live). Students could enter calls in the training environment without affecting the live system. In the event of a major incident, the training room served as the emergency operations center (EOC) or a back-up dispatch.

On the other end of the spectrum, thanks to active lobbying by the Denise Amber Lee Foundation and Rep. Ken Roberson, in 2009 the State of Florida passed a mandate requiring newly hired 911 call-takers and dispatchers to have 232 hours (5.8 weeks) of training *before* (emphasis mine) they are allowed to handle a 911 call. Those hired prior to that date had to take a competency exam; any failing the test would then need to take the training. The actual law went in to effect in October of 2012 and was supposed to be funded by the 911 tax.

The Lee family campaigned for mandatory dispatcher training after their family suffered a needless death. Denise Amber Lee was a kidnap victim who was found buried in a shallow grave two days after she was taken. Allegations of the call being mishandled by a Public Safety Answering Point spurred her family to declare that the outcome never happen to another kidnap victim again. One key concern made by Peggy and Mark Lee, which has been echoed by many dispatchers, is whether agencies will follow-through and do the training.

The State of Michigan added mandatory training for Public Safety Telecommunicators as of December of 2012. The State of Michigan now requires dispatchers to have 40 hours of initial training in their first 18 months, another 40 hours before their 24th month and then 24 hours of continuing education every two years afterwards. There is no certification involved, but every education requirement is a foundation to build on.

I wish could explain why society requires hair stylists and massage therapists to have minimal training hours but those answering 911 don't. Our neighbor to the north has offered a degree in emergency communications for some time. Dispatcher courses are few and far between, and those in existence often ride on the backs of law enforcement.

In many states, training depends upon the specific job of the Telecommunicators. For example: those handling emergency medical dispatching (EMD) must take and pass a certification course within a specified time frame from the first day on the job.

What is Your Emergency? The History of Public Safety Dispatching in America

Emergency Medical Dispatching requires annual re-certification, much like any other medical professional. Peace Officers Standards & Training (POST) certifies & train law enforcement officers, and in some states, the state agency also manages the certification and training of of law enforcement dispatchers. If a law enforcement agency agrees to follow POST regulations, and that state has standards in place for dispatchers, then the department agrees to follow the regulations for the dispatchers. Remember, generally POST certifications for dispatchers are voluntary. POST classes for dispatchers can include basic dispatcher, civilian training officer (CTO), civilian supervisor, active shooter events, crisis negotiations, tactical dispatcher, school violence, wellness, high risk events, and suicidal callers.

As an avid voice for training, I can't say enough for training dispatchers, whether it is at the entry level or for laterals. Again, an entry level dispatcher starts the job without any prior telecommunicator experience in law enforcement, firefighting, or emergency medical services whereas a lateral level dispatcher has worked in the public safety telecommunicator profession (emergency medical service, law enforcement, or fire) prior to taking the current position. Dispatchers who train other dispatchers are called Civilian Training Officers, or CTOs, and those personnel should be certified just as their equivalent in law enforcement.

Medium to large agencies may have formal dispatcher academies. In these cases, dispatcher trainees attend a class with other new hires where an instructor teaches the basics of the agency's policies and procedures. One learns criminal codes; geography; radio codes; call-taking; computer-aided dispatching; major incidents; various local, county, state, and national computerized data systems; and (if appropriate), fire, police, and emergency medical dispatching. When the classroom portion is complete, one is assigned to a civilian training officer for one-on-one live training. Training may be broken down to phases: call-taking, fire, telecommunications (inquiries, entries, updates of data bases), and police.

The telecommunication system consists of various hot file data bases (stolen vehicles, properties, missing and/or wanted persons, boats, securities, etc.) and criminal history among others. Not all agencies have access to all of the systems: it strictly depends of each department's needs. Access to the Federal Bureau of Information (FBI) data bases can be inquiry only, limited entry access, or full access depending upon the department's needs. One State agency is designated as the control authority and liason to the federal government. Each participating agaency must designate a coordinator and an IT person to train and monitor access & activity (more on this later).

During the training, dispatcher trainees might ride along with field personnel. Accompanying a field unit for a shift is an excellent experience to learn the covered jurisdiction, to see first-hand what 'the other side does', and hear radio traffic from the other end. Viewing the entire process of a traffic stop, a medical call, or how field sobriety testing is handled definitely helps a dispatcher to mentally picture what is going on later when he/she is behind the radio later on in the training. In medium to larger agencies, trainees may be required to go out on multiple rides with police units, fire, and emergency service personnel on a monthly or quarterly basis. If there is an opportunity to go out on a flight, take advantage of this and do it. Helicopter patrols area a great way to see your department's jurisdiction.

Trainers and trainees should track the progress in some written form. Large agencies generally have a formal process in place, but the mid to smaller departments may not have specific paperwork. As a new Public Safety Telecommunicator, documenting what policies & procedures (P&Ps) have been reviewed is important. One form which might be used is called a Daily Observation Report (DOR). Daily Observation Reports, or Weekly Observation Reports (WORs) should include any skills and/or knowledge reviewed that particular shift, tests given (with results), ride-alongs done (with whom and where), radio channels worked, significant calls taken, any problems (and how handled) or excellent events, and narrative sections for both trainer and trainee. Any significant issues with calls and/or radio traffic should have attachments in the form of radio tapes and CAD print-outs. DORs or WORs become a permanent part of a trainee's record.

What is Your Emergency? The History of Public Safety Dispatching in America

Dispatch trainees will have good and bad days. Civilian Training Officers should discuss each shift with the dispatch trainee. What went wrong or why was one shift excellent over the average one? Training documentation should be factual and not include any surprises. Trainers need to include supporting paperwork for any poor or superior performances, which may be copies of calls (Computer-Aided Dispatch incidents) and/or tapes of phone calls or radio traffic, and statements from co-workers. If a trainee is having continued difficulties, a final evaluation period on a contract may be initiated. During this specified time frame, a different trainer may be assigned. At the end of the training cycle, all three persons should sit down, either as a group or trainer with supervisor and trainee with supervisor, to review the overall performance. A decision on whether to move on or terminate will be made.

This is not an easy decision. If the choice is made to let the dispatch trainee go, a full explanation should be given as to why. Again, by this point, all parties should be aware of the status and the outcome most likely be expected.

NFPA and PSAPs

The National Fire Protection Association (NFPA) released its fire statistics for fire departments through the year 2010 on March 2012 and part of the information included data on 911 in the fire service. For example, from 2001 to 2010, the percentage of U.S. fire department with access to the internet went from 58% to 84%. That is significant because many of the new dispatch firefighter technologies (dispatch, training, investigation) are internet based. The study also noted in 2001 25% of fire departments had basic 911 service in 2010. 69% had enhanced 911 in 2001 and 75% used the enhanced version in 2010. Finally, 6% had no 911 service in 2001 while 1% still had no 911 in 2010. In 2001 only 39% of the fire departments didn't back-up dispatch centers while 35% didn't have them in 2010.

When it came to having their own dispatch, the NFPA statistics revealed 9% of fire departments had their own communications center in 2001, 33% were handled by a law enforcement agency (via a combined PSAP), 34% were dispatched by a public safety department, 2% were handled by a private company, and 23% by some other arrangement. In 2010, the numbers changed to show 5% of the fire departments with their own dispatch, 27% through the law enforcement, 42% by a public safety dispatch, 1% via a private company, and 25% via some other arrangement.

The trend of regional communications centers is growing. The federal government is encouraging all branches of public safety to join forces and merge small department dispatch centers together to save money. There are pros and cons on both methods. Smaller, individual centers allow dispatchers to know response districts and the personnel. When an in-progress event comes in, that dispatcher most likely knows exactly where the incident is from personal experience. Field personnel are recognized by voice. Local Telecommunicators keep their jobs. When agencies combine resources, personnel must either move to keep jobs or find another occupation. Regional Center Telecommunicators may not know the response jurisdictions as well as local dispatchers did, possibly delaying responders while the location is ascertained. Regional dispatchers may not be as familiar with the voices and habits of the First Responders, which could cost critical seconds in an in-progress event.

Integrated police and fire services, a true "Public Safety' agency, is one in which a few firefighter personnel are assigned to the stations as drivers for the equipment. The majority of the staff are cross-trained as law enforcement/firefighters. During the majority of the shift, the field personnel handle law enforcement duties until a fire or medical call comes in. At that point, they 'change hats' and respond to deal with the fire or emergency medical incident as First Responders. After the fire event or medical call is completed, the driver takes the fire apparatus back to the station and the rest of the field units return back to handling law enforcement events. Ambulance service is most likely contracted to a private provider for advanced life support service

What is Your Emergency? The History of Public Safety Dispatching in America

and transportation. All personnel respond for major incidents and fire suppression.

Agencies wishing to cut costs can contract the communications to a larger department or the county. Some areas pool their resources, creating a county-wide dispatch for both law enforcement and fire, combined or separate dispatch centers. Traditionally law enforcement serves as the primary Public Safety Answering Point, taking the 91-1 calls and transferring any requests for fire or emergency medical calls to the secondary center.

The actual duties of a Public Safety Dispatcher vary as much as the job title. Public Safety Answering Points (PSAPs) can be a single service – law enforcement only, or combined to handle all three branches – law, fire and emergency medical services. Not every department provides the pre-arrival medical instructions (emergency medical dispatching, or EMD).

Wants and Warrants: NCIC and the TAC

Today, the use of a computer-aided dispatch (CAD) system is the normal operating method of tracking field unit status and calls for service. Law enforcement units inquire on the status of persons, vehicles, boats, gun, property and other items as part of their jobs. Dispatch personnel access various data bases via the Department of Justice National Criminal Information Center's (NCIC) computers, managed by the Federal Bureau of Investigation (FBI). The NCIC was developed in 1965 by the FBI, a brilliant concept of investigative sharing for law enforcement agencies. The intent was a network of information instantly available to the field personnel.

NCIC is available 24 hours a day to authorized users. There are three levels of access for users of NCIC: inquiry only, limited entry, and full entry. Inquiry only agencies do not perform any entries to the local, state, or national system data bases. The departments can send teletype requests to verify a warrant, send a message to other agencies, or locate a missing person or stolen property. Another, usually a contracted department, handles any warrant entries for that agency. Limited access refers to a department that can enter towed/stored vehicles and a few other transactions according to their needs. The full-access allows dispatchers to enter records, update, locate, and clear entries. Agencies can also enter Amber Alerts, which is an abduction alert notification system when a child is taken (certain criteria must be met before an entry of child abduction can be made in the Amber Alert System).

Each agency must perform a fingerprint-based state and federal background check on a user prior to any access to the system. Each state is responsible for following Department of Justice rules, and for setting rules for the state computerized systems. In addition, individual counties may have their own local data bases. Any agency granted access must designate a Terminal Agency Coordinator, or TAC, to oversee that department's training, certification, and audits. TACs may designate as many Assistant Terminal Agency Coordinators (ATACs) as necessary to help with the duties. Each agency must also have a Local Agency Security Officer (LASO) to handle the computer programming, networking, and technical security, or IT, duties.

What is Your Emergency? The History of Public Safety Dispatching in America

Chapter Seven: How the Public Perceives Us

Before television, Americans listened to radio. One popular program was a show called *Calling All Cars:* This broadcast program took real cases from the Los Angeles Police and fictionalized them. The show started out with a Public Safety Telecommunicator putting out a broadcast. This dispatcher, Jesse Rosenquist, was a real dispatcher for the LAPD. The broadcast then switched to the LAPD Chief, James E. Davis who gave a brief introduction to the weeks' crime, similar to Rod Sterling's Twilight Zone beginning monologue.

Just the facts: Dragnet, Emergency! and Adam-12

Jack Webb was a genius when it came to creating realistic public safety dramas. Every drama relating to fire, police, or emergency medical services owes him thanks for setting the bar. Jack's landmark show was *Dragnet,* where he played Joe Friday, a Los Angeles police Detective. Made famous for his, 'Just the facts' catch-phrase, *Dragnet,* used a real Los Angeles police dispatcher for some episodes. That dispatcher, Shaaron Claridge, later was cast as the voice of the dispatcher for *Adam-12.* Shaaron and her fire counterpart, Sam Lanier, are probably two of the most famous dispatchers in our profession.

Samuel Lanier Jr., was a Los Angeles County Fire Department dispatcher for *Emergency!* Every week, viewers would hear Sam tone out and dispatch Engine 51 and Squad 51 to fires, rescues, and medical calls all over Los Angeles County. Footage of the dispatch center showed Sam at his console, busy at work. Sam worked the 'A' shift for the LA County Fire Dispatch. Sam joined the LACO FD in 1958 as a Dispatcher and worked until his retirement in 1977. During an interview, Sam said he made up the locations used for squad 51 by combining streets that didn't normally cross, adding extra numbers to streets, or even making up a few street names. After Sam retired in 1977, he did consulting for TV and film productions. Tragically, he died of a heart attack while trying to help victims of an accident close to his home.

Two of Sam's co-workers occasionally joined him on the radio, or in the background. Duane Lewis was often seen helping out Sam on the dispatch footage. Duane was a firefighter/dispatcher on the 'A' shift, eventually trading in his headset to transfer to the field. He retired in 2003, as a fire captain. Lanny Cunningham worked the 'B' shift as a firefighter/dispatcher and also helped out on occasion when on an overtime shift.

Producer Jack Webb wanted his new police drama, *Adam-12*, to have as much realism as possible, just like *Emergency!* depicted. He hired Shaaron Claridge to come on board to provide the voice-overs for *Adam-12*. Her calm voice was part of the opening radio monologue for each show, and she played the dispatcher role in nineteen episodes. In the fifth season, episode 20, entitled *Suspended*, Shaaron had a short walk-on role. Her face was artfully blocked by camera angles, so to keep her appearance hidden and preserve her anoniminity. In California, dispatchers are granted the same confidentiality as law enforcement officers in order to prevent retaliation by disgruntled members of society. As with Sam in *Emergency!*, Jack would occasionally show the communications center to heighten the excitement. Shaaron also provided the radio voice for *Colombo and Lou Grant*.

Be careful out there: Law Enforcement on the television

Steve Bocchio's *Hill Street Blues* didn't show the dispatchers but the television audience heard the voices over the radio. Called one of the best, grittiest, most realistic police dramas produced to date, *Hill Street Blues* pushed the limits and went where no police show had ever gone before. The 'employees' of the Hill weren't glamorous, had everyday problems, and could have been anyone's partners. No city was actually named as the home of Hill Street, although viewers would put odds on the location being Chicago. The show began each episode with a shift briefing by Sgt. Phil Esterhaus. After he finished going over the latest crime sprees, talked about any department issues, and went one-on-one with a couple of the cops, he always ended the meeting with the trademark, "And let's be careful out there."

What is Your Emergency? The History of Public Safety Dispatching in America

COPS is a reality show about the law enforcement officers in the field, but one can't have patrol without Public Safety Telecommunicators. Every officer on *Cops* uses a radio, whether it is to call in a contact, acknowledge a call, request a backup, or to request an inequity check. Viewers don't see the dispatchers but the voices are heard *every* show doing their job.

Alaska State Troopers followed the law enforcement officers as they patrolled both highways and back country areas of Alaska. Alaska Troopers deal with all facets of enforcement, including wildlife, search & rescue, and criminal activity. Dispatchers are heard interacting with the officers.

60 Minutes news has turned an eye on public safety, with at least one episode focusing on public safety telecommunications. Too bad, the episodes didn't focus on the positives on our field. Many of the short stories focus on the negative aspects of dispatching, such as delayed call response or poor outcomes due to dispatcher errors.

Reno 911 a campy faux reality show following the make-believe Reno Sheriff, the dispatchers are heard in the background over the radio.

240-Robert: was a short-lived show focusing on the Los Angeles County Sheriff's Search and Rescue division. The program actually had a dispatcher role cast to the program.

Wild Justice, North Woods Law and Rugged Justice are reality shows have become popular on recently and focus on the fish and game end of law enforcement. Game Wardens patrol and enforce laws relating to natural resources (hunting, fishing, and habitat). More often than not wardens work by themselves in remote areas but they can also be seen in large cities, waterways, and coastal areas. Fish and wildlife enforcement officers have the same powers as any street officer.

The list of law enforcement dramas is long and deserves a book of its own. For that reason, I'm not listing most of them. Most of the shows would have radio traffic in the background at one point or another. The same goes for fire dramas.

by Diana Sprain

You're doing it wrong: Trauma's 'Crossed Wires' episode

Trauma was a short-lived drama set in San Francisco centering on the fire-rescue personnel of the San Francisco Department of Public Safety. Although the television program focused on the life flight helicopter and ambulance personnel, radio traffic was heard through-out the field portion of each episode. One particular show, entitled 'Crossed Wires' focused on a day when the dispatch center's computer had a meltdown. After an incident in which a patient dies due to an extended eta, the angry crew drives to the Communications Center to confront the Public Safety Telecommunicator who handled the call.

The Dispatch Supervisor heads off the medic, who handled the patient care, thinking on her feet and tries to explain the problem. She puts the medic at a dispatch console at a quick suggestion of a line dispatcher, who offers her headset to the disgruntled paramedic. Between the Supervisor, and two dispatchers, the medic handles one call: a man speaking in Russian, reporting his child bitten by his neighbor's dog. The male is threatening to shoot the dog. Without getting any details, he 'knows' what ambulance to dispatch and hangs up on the caller after telling the translator (called by the back-up dispatcher behind him) a couple of quick medical instructions. He is prompted to call the police to respond, and then again to call animal control. He proudly announces how that wasn't so hard. The Supervisor tells him the combined response time is 30 minutes for all the agencies involved.

This episode was criticized for what the Dispatch Supervisor *didn't say or do*. The call involved a threat, which was never followed through. The 'police' side didn't ask any questions. In reality, if a dispatcher took such a call, yes an ambulance, law enforcement, and animal control would have all responded BUT, the reporting party would have been queried on the gun, descriptions of involved parties obtained and that information relayed to the responding law enforcement units.

As the episode progressed, and radio traffic had problems, dispatch would have made allowances for the computer-aided dispatch (CAD) and had a back-up system in place. Just as important, no one would accept dispatchers and field personnel arguing on the air. To say 'we don't know where you are' is an insult to every Public Safety Telecommunicator on the job. There are always methods to track field units' status. Finally, Communications Centers are generally secure areas, allowing access to authorized personnel only. To think that a crew, especially an angry crew, would be allowed open access inside a communications center which is generally a secure area to confront a dispatcher as portrayed in this episode, is unthinkable. Complaints are handled via a chain-of-command. Finally, the medic would have *sat with* a dispatcher, not *in place of a dispatcher*.

Multiple shows have been set in the firefighting realm, *Rescue Me,* Dennis Leary's ode to firefighters and *Chicago Fire* have radio traffic as part of the show but only as part of the background. One older show, *Rescue 8* might be called the precursor to *Emergency!*.

Dispatchers on the Big Screen

Mother, Juggs, & Speed starring Bill Cosby, Raquel Welch, and Harvey Keitel in this 1976 cult film about a private ambulance company competing with another ambulance service for a lucrative county contract while dealing with a slew of kooky employees. Raquel, the company dispatcher, informs the boss she has finished her Emergency Medical Technician course and wants to make the switch from dispatcher to working on the ambulance. The antics of the field crew include call jumping from a scanner, sabotage of the rival companies' units, and even accidentally setting fire to their own station. Despite the outrageous comedy, the movie does have its serious moments, when a crewmember is shot & killed by a drug-seeking junkie. Many of the parodied events are known to have happened in the smaller companies during the time frame of the mid 70's to early 80's.

Crazy Mary and Dirty Larry is a 1974 action film in which the majority of the film is one big car chase. The local dispatcher and the Sheriff spend time coordinating units in the attempt to stop the villains in this film.

The *Die Hard series* character poor John McClane always seems to find himself in trouble. Each film does feature dispatch in one form or another. The first film uses dispatchers more than any of the others, especially in the first part. In *Live Free or Die Hard,* the bad guys pretend to be dispatchers until 'John McClane' uses a radio code to confuse them.

1999's *Bringing Out the Dead* was one of those films that only sense to those in the public safety profession and left the public scratching their heads unless they read the book before seeing the film first. Queen Latifah and Martin Scorsese played the dispatcher roles, giving the EMTs and paramedics the right amount of snark mixed in with the normal radio traffic to make it realistic.

Striking Distance another Bruce Willis film showed dispatchers for the Pittsburgh River Rescue Patrol near the beginning of the film working in the Public Safety Answering Point (911 PSAP), wearing uniforms in a very nice Communications Center. Primary dispatcher 'Kim Lee' had a minor role, interacting with Bruce's character, filling out the dispatch schedule and working the radio channel.

Beverly Hills Cop had a couple of scenes in a Communications Center of the 'Beverly Hills Police Department'. The dispatcher, who appears to be a sworn officer, uses an old-fashioned console to look up information and put out radio broadcasts. When the camera pans across the room, one can see large maps, video displays, and other equipment used by the dispatch personnel.

Dispatching's first feature film: The Call

The Call was released in March of 2013 and was widely anticipated by Public Safety Telecommunicators. The film ran 96 minutes and focuses on Jordan Turner, a Los Angeles Police Department 911 Call-Taker (she answers to 'operator' in the film). The call-taking center is referred as 'The Hive' which was the original name of the movie, but was changed (as Hollywood often does). The movie starts out with Jordan dealing with a mistake: She takes a burglary call from a teenager. After her caller disconnects the line, Jordan calls back the teenager who is hiding from the invader. The suspect hears the phone ring as he is searching the house. Finding the terrified girl hiding under a bed, he subsequently kidnaps & kills the victim.

Six months later, Jordan is taking dispatch trainees on a tour when another call resembling the same type of incident that sent Jordan to the training division comes in to a dispatcher recently released on her own. Jordan ends up taking over 'the call'. The majority of the movie is Jordan staying on the line with a kidnapping victim, until the girl loses the phone connection. Jordan makes it her mission to find the girl before the killer takes her life. The role of the public safety telecommunicator is well represented and believable up to the point when Halle Berry leaves the communications center to track down the kidnapper. At the end of the movie, the killer/kidnapper is left tied to a chair below ground by the rescued girl and Jordan. The killer recognizes Jordan's voice and comments that she is the operator. Instead of responding back with, "No, I am a Public Safety Telecommunicator." Jordan just says yes and the movie ends.

Dispatchers on the World Wide Web

Live internet radio broadcasts have become almost as popular as scanners. Where the scanners have the ability to scan multiple channels on various frequencies, so do internet broadcasts. The primary differences between the two being internet connections can pick up more than the local departments, not being restricted to distance. Internet radio broadcasts may require membership to access full services.

Internet magazines There are many subscription-only and web-only magazines dedicated to Public Safety. *Dispatch Monthly* started out as a print/internet newsletter and later changed to an internet only format. This site was run by former Public Safety Dispatcher (and Reserve Berkeley Police - CA) Officer) Gary Allen. Dispatch Monthly posted daily tidbits, a newsletter, and the

by Diana Sprain

online site has facts, history, job postings, a tape log of incidents, and dispatch boards (requires registration to participate). Sadly, the live site went dark after Gary retired due to an illness (he passed away in 2015). Supporters have since put the website back up as an archieved site. The references and audio files are available for use.

APCO, Firehouse Magazine, JEMS Magazine, and many other Public Safety magazines have websites with access to the current and back-issues. In addition to the magazine, each offers social media boards for their readers which do require registration before one can access that feature.

Web blogs are all the rage. Many dispatch-related or Public Safety web blogs are available on the web. *911 Cares, Dispatch Fire1, EMS1,* and, *Police1*. These sites offer information, articles, social media boards, emailed newsletters, and classified ads (including job postings).

Print magazines come in two varieties: member news and individual journals. National Emergency Number of America (NENA) publishes a magazine which is a benefit of membership. *The Call* (no relation to the movie of the same name) includes Association news, legislative news, dispatch articles, and NENA Chapter news. The Association of Public Safety Communications Officials, International, Inc. (APCO) publishes a magazine every month as a benefit of its membership. This magazine, *Public Safety Communications,* includes Association news, training articles, major incident briefings, information from vendors, Chapter news, regular columns, and continuing education articles for certified dispatchers. The International Academies of Emergency Dispatch (IAED) publishes *The Journal of Emergency Dispatch* which has continuing education articles, news, dispatcher tips, and current events.

The Public Safety realm incorporates three primary areas as we have learned: law enforcement, fire, and emergency medical services. Each of these services has national associations which have trade journals. In addition, magazines like the Journal of Emergency Medical Services (JEMS) Magazine and Firehouse Magazine often feature articles on dispatching. There are many publications available to the law enforcement community and many of those include the occasional article on dispatching.

911 Magazine

911 Magazine's first issue was published in the winter of 1988 by Jim Voelkl, whose family owned the publishing firm of Official Publishing, Inc. (OPI). OPI already was known for other Public Safety magazines in the general field such as *Firehouse*, *JEMS*, and *Police Chief*. 911 Magazine's first issue was only 36 pages containing several articles, advertisements, and illustrations. The next issue was the Spring 1989, which included some color photographs and more articles. By the fall issue, the magazine had changed from a quarterly format to bi-monthly, with glossy paper and more photographs. The Loma-Prieta earthquake was the feature story.

Randall Larson wrote about the history of the magazine in 1999. In the editorial piece he explains the origins of the journal, "Jim Voelkl initially served as both editor and publisher, with page design by Lori Loucks. Jim's wife Richele served as the magazine's Systems Manager, insuring the necessary behind-the-scenes tasks were accomplished to get the magazine out. Jim's mother Jackie, co-founder of OPI in 1945, came aboard as the magazine's Public Information Officer. A frequent traveler, Jackie would often write articles about public safety agencies in the places she visited… Jul/Aug 90 was a milestone in the magazine's appearance. Completely revamped by Lil Fox, our new Art Director, this issue featured our new 3-color logo and the cover format we've used throughout the decade. The magazine's focus continued to be toward the future – reporting on significant incidents handled by public safety while looking ahead at trends, technology, and techniques that will affect the emergency response community. We started three regular columns – Police (Martin C, Brhel, Jr.), EMS (J. Franaszek, D. Lemak & J. Ratko), and Communications (Martin Stilman)."

"The magazine continued to grow. The increased use of feature articles with color photos focused on dispatch issues. 9-1-1 didn't shy away from hot topics, including the new technologies of GIS, next generation 9-1-1, and training. The renowned Alan Burton joined the staff beginning with the May/June 1991 issue. San Jose dispatcher Randall Larson joined the editorial staff on 1993 as did regular contributor Berkeley Police dispatcher Gary Allen. With the Nov/Dec. 1994 Gary Allen became an Associate Editor – good job, Gary! Randall was promoted to Editor in the winter of 1995 when Alan Burton moved on to other projects. 9-1-1 Magazine just became better, with expanded articles on major incidents, communications centers, and training. Alas, all good things must change with the times. Circumstances dictated the magazine move in a different direction, with the print format going away and the magazine changing to an on-line version only as it stands today.

Chapter Eight: 911 on Television

Rescue 911 saves lives

On the 8th December 1989, the President of CBS television, Kim LeMasters was driving to work. As with many of the residents of Los Angeles, he drove to work listening to CBS News, especially, "The Osgood File' with Charles Osgood. It was fate that had Mr. LeMasters listening when Osgood re-broadcast a recording of a home invasion. The call was chilling. A family at home had their lives forever changed when a man broke in and attacked the father. The fourteen year old son shot the suspect while the 911 line was still open, killing the man.

Mr. LeMasters was intrigued and excited. The entire sequence had him mesmerized. He wanted to hear more. There definitely was potential for a television special. He contacted his President of CBS Productions, Norman Powell. A decision was made to find a producer and produce two or three shows as soon as possible.

On Friday, January the 13th, 1989, Norman Powell contacted Arnold Shapiro. Mr. Shapiro was known for his Oscar winning documentary *("Sacred Straight"*) Normally, a producer would go to the studios to pitch an idea for a television special or series. In this case, Norman called Arnold and asked if he was interested in producing the project and how fast did he think it might take?

"I'll be there in twenty minutes to discuss the project with you." Arnold replied. "3 specials were proposed. That day he (Norman) offered me the specials. No format, no host. NO 'reality' was really developed yet (until *"Survivor"*); the other program on the air that was close was America Most Wanted which came out same year." explained Mr. Shapiro during a phone interview with the author of this book.

Mr. Shapiro and Mr. Powell were very enthusiastic about this yet unnamed television show. It had to be exciting enough to catch the public's attention and contain enough reality to make the show interesting. They decided on a combination documentary format, which allowed them to use the real involved parties along with recreated events of the emergency.

"When we shot the footage of the emergency, we had stunt professionals & actors perform instead of the actual victims. We couldn't have the real victims involved in the shooting of the incident. The emotional trauma was too much to ask of them. The radio and telephone recordings were used as is with one change: the dispatchers lip-synched as best they could to make it episode look as if it were happening right now."

It was decided to highlight four stories for each the special. According to Mr. Shapiro, each tale was selected according to different factors which included the feasibility of the story, the appropriateness for television, and on occasion he even allowed a story when someone died provided the heroism was spectacular, and balance (medical verses technical rescues or crime stories). I tried to mix stories for episodes (4 tales – 1 documentary / 3 re-creations. The material for the show was gathered from newspaper blurbs, magazines, and the news. The show staff contacted police, fire, emergency medical services, and emergency rooms to inquire on potential stories. Mr. Shapiro said he wasn't aware that NENA, APCO, or the many trade journals existed.

With the format of the show set, the next step was to hire a celebrity host. CBS President LeMasters suggested Leonard Nimoy. Mr. Nimoy had narrated many documentaries, as well as being known for his *Star Trek* fame. Arnold came back with his choice of William Shatner. "I'd already worked with him on two prior projects."

A busy man, Shatner had a law enforcement 'connection' through his previous work in the series *TJ Hooker*. Shatner was busy, working on a film but the new, unnamed show's filming schedule was able to adjust the filming schedule to accommodate the star. He signed on for the specials. Shatner's on camera segments were shot at Oxnard Police Department's Communications Center.

The first special was scheduled for release in April 1989 and the second in May. *Rescue 911* was a success, each show winning its time slot. CBS was thrilled. Instead of televising the third special in June, the executives scheduled "*Rescue 911*" as a regular series beginning in the fall. The third special became the seventh

What is Your Emergency? The History of Public Safety Dispatching in America

episode of the new series. Mr. Shatner worked twice a month to film his on-camera sequences for the show. On Sundays, he was taped at the Huntington Beach Police Department's Communications Center to film the lead-ins and on Fridays he was in LA to tape the narrations. Huntington Beach was selected because the crew had access to dispatch, police, fire, and ambulances all at the same place.

Sundays were the 'quietest' shifts. Alas, as we know, public safety is a fickle business and the director had to stop shooting when real calls interrupted Shatner's work. Mr. Shapiro said, "If we had known we were going to last for seven seasons, we'd have built a set recreating the Huntington Beach Dispatch and hired actors to portray dispatchers. That would have allowed us to film at any time."

With the series ordered, Shapiro set his staff to find dramatic 911 calls. As the show continued, viewers and public safety started submitting material. "Half of the submissions received were not usable (too gruesome, unsafe, too expansive, not 'PC', etc.). Only two or three out of 20 were seriously considered for the show." Meanwhile, William Shatner handled the PR, spreading the word about the new television show as only he could.

As the seasons progressed, Arnold created the occasional 'theme' episode. One of the more popular shows involved animals saving people. Another theme was a funniest calls show which included a burglar on Christmas Eve who tried to climb down a chimney head first and became stuck; a burglar who entered a building through a skylight and then was unable to leave and called 911 to be rescued; and a boy who managed to get his tongue stuck in freezer.

When asked about *Rescue 911*, Mr. Shapiro couldn't have been any more proud as he talked what the show meant to him and the public.

"One of our stories saved the life of a family (a couple and 4 children) in St Louis. The dad was moving items from their old house to their new one. He had lit the furnace while the mom and kids were putting things away at the new house. She started feeling ill and became worse. He ended up taking her to local emergency room, leaving the kids at the new house. While they were waiting in the emergency room, they saw *Rescue 911* on the television in the waiting room. The episode dealt with CO_2 poisoning. Both parents suddenly recognized the symptoms; Dad raced home to check on the kids and found his children unconscious or semi-conscious. If he hadn't seen the show and gone home to check on the children, they would have succumbed to carbon monoxide poisoning."

"There were so many great shows over the seasons. The viewers watched and learned from the segments. People wrote us about how they used those lessons to help others. We did a 100 lives saved episode (two independent sources verified the 'saves'). CBS was amazed. In 7 ½ years we did three specials 100/ 220/300 lives saved. A total of 350 total lives saved at the end of series. People paid attention to 'Stop, drop & roll', installing smoke detectors, not putting electrical cord under rugs, how to use the Heimlich maneuver, etc. and actually put that knowledge to use to save a life. We're proud of that."

Reminiscing, Mr. Shapiro said, "I've produced 29 series and Rescue 911 is my favorite. It is one of the most important series I've made and a worthwhile show because of what it taught people. I know that it is responsible for many young men and women becoming 911 dispatchers, paramedics, firefighters, or law enforcement officers. When the show was on the air, it was a top twelve. I have to say that was in part due to the hard work and dedication of the 100+ people on my production team. I couldn't have done it without them."

Other 911 Reality Shows

Call 911: the next generation of television dispatchers
In 2008 through 2011, another show hit the airwaves based upon the *Rescue 911* format. Tom Jennings produced the show which aired in 2008 and 2009; with 60 episodes completed and shown. *Call 911* used a similar style of recordings, interviews, and reenactments to tell stories of emergencies.

Panic 911: Third time around the block

What is Your Emergency? The History of Public Safety Dispatching in America

Debuted in 2012 and cancelled in 2013, Siren Media's *Panic 911* was another show highlighting the public safety events starting from the initial 911 call to the resolution of the event. A total of nine episodes aired of what was supposed to be an edgy new series on the interaction between Public Safety Telecommunicators, the public, and First Responders.

Outrageous 911: A two-part series released by TLC on December 14, 2013, this documentary produced by Mike Mathis Productions was advertised to be about non-emergency incidents called in on the three-digit number.

What's Next?

Will there be other shows to focus on Public Safety Telecommunicators? Rescue 911 is a tough act to follow. My only complaint with any of these shows was how dispatch looked when it was filmed. I'm sorry, but how many communications centers have fresh flowers? Most of us aren't coming to work in freshly pressed uniforms or clothing or wearing flawless makeup. We're human. We all have our good days and bad. Personally, I prefer wearing uniforms but my current department doesn't require that of us unless we go to a meeting outside of dispatch. Not to mention the occasional rough language heard when the phone is disconnected or radio silent. Yes folks, we vent – some more than others.

Usually, our desks have mishmash of water bottles, paperwork, maybe a magazine or book, or a cell phone scattered about. We all personalized the workstations to some extent. You just didn't see that on the television shows. Silly I know, but go to enough public safety dispatch centers and you'll understand what I'm talking about.

Chapter Nine: Dispatcher Standards: Building the bar but where are the standards?

"America Deserves Better"

"In April 2009, the Association of Public-Safety Communication Officials International (APCO) established a task force to specifically review human resource challenges affecting 911 Public Safety Communication Centers (PSCC) across the country. In 2010, at the APCO International Conference held in Houston, Texas, an interim report was published by the task force which took into consideration and reported on all of the data collected which included a comprehensive review of state mandated training requirements, salary & benefits available to the men and women performing critical services to all communities in this country and provided a national grade based upon the information collected. The initial report reflected an overall grade based upon the information available at its publication. A year later, there has been some progress, but the progress is still insufficient to consistently, comprehensively, and sufficiently support the critical mission and public safety communications professionals. The overall grade remains at an F." William D. Carrow, President, APCO, Inc, 2009.

What is APCO, and why did Mr. Carrow's words matter to any person working in Public Safety?

One must go back to January of 1935 in St. Louis, Missouri, where police Sergeant Everett Fisher and Louis Padberg discussed the possibility of a national organization dedicated to advancing the cause of law enforcement radio. On January 21rst of that year, the two men, and 28 representatives from other agencies met to hammer out a fledgling organization: the Associated Police Communications Officers, or APCO. The main focus of the first meeting was to discuss three particular issues: FCC regulations, exchange of ideas, and, standards for police dispatching. A date for the next year's conference was set in Indianapolis and a newsletter typed up. That second meeting held in 1936 had 90 attendees.

What is Your Emergency? The History of Public Safety Dispatching in America

Every consecutive year thereafter, the number of men showing up at the APCO conference grew. In 1938, APCO officers started encouraging the establishment of local (state) chapters. The association released a list of 10-codes in 1939, the same year the organization incorporated. It is curious at first that the majority of high-level leaders were men in the early years until one considers the overall make-up of law enforcement (a male-dominated profession).

The Association of Police Communications Officers became involved in coordinating emergency communications during World War I. APCO welcomed other public safety disciplines in 1960. In 1982, APCO and the Illinois Chapter, at the Bradley University Library, came to an agreement to set up a permanent historical document collection. APCO established the APCO Institute, a dispatcher training division, in 1988. APCO championed the Public Safety Telecommunicators Week and Congress approved this declaration in 1991. The celebration was initiated by the Contra Costa County Sheriffs (CA) in 1981. In 2004, APCO released the 911 Commission Report, an intensive study of 911 within the United States.

APCO has been involved in training and education via special projects since the 1960's. Mobile communications had stretched the availability of the frequencies set aside for Public Safety. The first project, 'Project 1" was launched to spread the word about the shortage of frequency allocation. By getting out the word in the form of handouts, a color film, and reporting use-cards, APCO meant to pressure the Federal Communications Commission to address the problem and free up additional space.

More projects were tabled, including Project 2 (Public Safety Communications Standard Operations Manual), Project 11 (Basic Radio Operator and Dispatcher training based upon Project 2), Project 14 (radio code study), Project 25 (standard for digital telecommunications technology), and Project 33 (National Public Safety Telecommunications Training Standard). Not all of APCO's projects have been successful. Project 6 was a filming of the 1970 National Conference. Instead of boosting attendance at further conventions and, selling copies of the film, the project failed. In later years, the Conferences have done better selling CD & DVDs after the seminars and festivities were over.

Today, the Associated Public Communications Officials, Inc. has chapters all over the world. The organization lobbies in Washington D.C. for laws favorable towards Public Safety. In addition to radio frequency allocation, APCO champions dispatchers and radio technicians. The original newsletter, The APCO Bulletin later changed to a magazine which was again renamed Public Safety Communications. The yearly conference is attended by thousands of members over a week in August, rotating locations within the continental US.

Dedicated to 911

The National Emergency Number Association website explains the organizations' purpose:

"As *The Voice of 9-1-1*™, NENA is on the forefront of all emergency communications issues. The association serves its members and the greater public safety community as the only professional organization solely focused on 9-1-1 policy, technology, operations, and education issues. With more than 7,000 members in 48 chapters across the United States and around the globe, NENA promotes the implementation and awareness of 9-1-1, as well as international three-digit emergency communications systems. NENA works with 9-1-1 professionals nationwide, public policy leaders, emergency services and telecommunications industry partners, like-minded public safety associations, and other stakeholder groups to develop and carry out critical programs and initiatives, to facilitate the creation of an IP-based Next Generation 9-1-1 system, and to establish industry leading standards, training, and certifications. Through the association's efforts to provide effective and efficient public safety solutions, NENA strives to protect human life, preserve property, and maintain the security of our communities."

What is the difference between NENA and APCO? APCO concerns itself with the entire realm of public safety communications (commercial, radio, technicians, and dispatch) whereas NENA focuses on the 911 dispatchers. NENA and APCO do work together on many projects and lobby together for legislation.

Emergency Medical Dispatching

After visiting King County (Seattle, WA) and seeing the success of the Medic One EMS including the dispatcher – involvement of the CPR program, a Utah physician wanted to begin a program in his own area. Dr. Jeff Clawson had a vision: begin the emergency treatment process from the moment the 911 line is answered, instead of waiting until the first responders arrive on scene. Why couldn't the process work? Dr. Clawson spent time working as a dispatcher and Emergency Medical Technician for Gold Cross Ambulance Service while going to medical school. He knew, as did many dispatchers, firefighters and emergency medical personnel, that lives could be saved if communications center personnel – the dispatchers – could provide some instruction.

The key was to come up with a program that was easy to use, standardize the training, and convince departments, dispatch personnel, and the field units that the system would work. Dr. Clawson filed his idea, determined to see what he could come up with. In 1978, Dr. Clawson introduced his emergency medical dispatch protocols. On the official website for the Academy of Emergency Medical Dispatch (AEMD) gives more explanation:

"Clawson designed a set of protocols that would standardize the way dispatchers communicated with callers and, in turn, improve the emergency response system. The original set of protocols published in 1978 contained 29 sets of two 8-inch-by-5-inch cards. Each caller complaint was listed in alphabetical order, as they are today, and reflected either a symptom (e.g., abdominal pain, burns, cardiac/respiratory arrest) or an incident (e.g., electrocutions, drowning, or traffic injury accident). The core card contained three color-coded areas: key questions, pre-arrival instructions, and dispatch priorities, and they were distributed on for the good of dispatch. "We gave away the cards just so they [the public safety agencies] would do something about their dispatch," Clawson said. The doctor believed in the protocol system, and he wanted others to share in the success of a well-coordinated response team that included dispatchers as the "first, first responders" - a phrase he coined in 1981 for the first national meeting that included emergency medical dispatch."

From one hundred departments and agencies in 1981 to well over 3000 to date in multiple countries, the Medical Priority Dispatch System is saving lives. The System branched out, adding law enforcement and fire protocols to its arsenal of dispatch systems.

The road to standards started with POST

Peace Officers Standards and Training, or POST, develops curriculum, standards, programs, and continuing education for law enforcement personnel. The programs may include training for communications center staff, as is the case with California. Compliance for dispatchers is dependent upon legislature: for example, law enforcement agencies accepting POST money to assist in covering the expense of a law enforcement recruit's academy training may be required to send their law enforcement dispatch staff to the basic Public Safety Dispatcher course.

Back in the late 1980's, California POST held a series of workshops throughout the State and invited dispatchers from as many departments as possible. In the workshops, the dispatch personnel brainstormed over job descriptions and duties. From those meetings, POST personnel came up with an updated job description and course for law enforcement Public Safety Dispatchers. The course went from 40 to 80 hours. In the 1990's, the program was updated again, going to 120 hours. It is important to remember, for all the training, the class focused on law enforcement with a basic over-view of fire & emergency medical services. Part of the problem in California, as it is with many states & agencies, is the variance in policies & procedures and radio codes. Instructors at the POST schools were required to have a degree, which eliminated many of the veteran dispatchers who who have made excellent instructors.

Law enforcement recruitment programs focus on sworn personnel, rarely including dispatchers. Explorer programs should have a dispatcher section. All field-training programs should require radio communications be taught by Civilian-Training Officer-certified dispatchers. Every community service meeting or meet & greet event should have a dispatcher available for general questions. High school education events with law enforcement or fire should include dispatchers. Any ems day should have EMD-trained dispatchers to educate the public. Public Safety Telecommunicators must get involved outside of the communications center to have a true voice.

Continuity across the board in training, regardless of a radio frequencies, computer-aided dispatch software, or departmental policies & procedures will truly make interoperability a reality. Can it be done? One can only hope. Dispatcher Managers should adopt the APCO/NENA training standards if none exist in their state.

Dispatchers helping dispatchers: TERT

In 2005 Hurricane Rita made landfall in Louisiana and Texas. The devastating storm taxed the abilities of the local public safety resources. Not only did the communications centers staff handle the problems resulting from the storm, many were personally impacted by the event. A call was sent through the government chain to request a multi-agency Telecommunicator Emergency Response Team (TERT) to provide relief for the dispatchers. What is TERT?

"In partnership, the National Emergency Number Association and the Association of Public Safety Communications Officials-International are dedicated to the development of a nationally recognized program for telecommunicator mutual aid response in the aftermath of disasters, providing information as to operational deployment of Telecommunicator Emergency Response Taskforce (TERT) programs and taking a leadership role in assisting governmental agencies in the development of TERT style programs at the regional, state and local levels."

The mission statement of the TERT program is simple: when rescuers need help and dispatchers are overwhelmed beyond the extraordinary, a call is sent out to bring in outside assistance. In the past, mutual aid requests during disasters brought in first responders: fire fighters, law enforcement, and emergency medical personnel, to deal with the immediate impact. In addition to the rescuers, public works, utilities, search & rescue, telecommunications (phones, satellites, & radio technicians), National Guard, Red Cross, and construction staff came in to help with the logistics of locating victims and the salvage operations. Despite the massive response of emergency responders there was one key area left out: the 911 centers. No one ever thought about the over-burdened Public Safety Telecommunicators.

Telecommunicators need only look to the example of the field personnel to see how successful a response team is. The Association for Public Safety Communications Officials, Inc (APCO) in conjunction with the National Emergency Number Association (NENA) released *the APCO/NENA ANSI Standard for the TERT Deployment 1.1051.2009* on May 27th, 2009. This document explains the basics of a TERT member, the process of a request, the call-out information required, and contains examples of equipment necessary for deployment. More states are jumping on the TERT bandwagon. It is comforting to know when a major event hits, dispatch resources can be requested, the same as for fire or law enforcement.

Mandatory Standards: Florida Law

One of the more recent states to jump on the mandatory Public Safety Telecommunicator training is the State of Florida. Title XXIX of the Public Health Law, section 401.465 *911 Public Safety Telecommunicator Certification* states:

"(a) Effective October 1, 2012, any person employed as a 911 public safety telecommunicator or at a public safety answering point, as defined in s. 365.172(3) (a), must be certified by the department."

"(b) A public safety agency, as defined in s. 365.171(3) (d), may employ a 911 public safety telecommunicator trainee for a period not to exceed 12 months of the trainee works under the direct supervision of a certified public safety telecommunicator, as determined by rile of the department, and is enrolled in a public safety communicator training program."

The wording of the law goes on to establish the requirement for training by the individual agencies, a requirement for dispatchers to complete a certification training program, for the dispatchers to swear an oath that they are not addicted to alcohol or controlled substances, and that they are free from mental or physical defects or diseases that would impair their ability to perform the job. The State certification is good for two years, requiring re-certification after that time frame.

What exactly does Florida say the Public Safety Telecommunicators must learn? What happens if they fail the re-certification class? Must unions and agencies re-write labor contracts to account for the new law? How many times can a Telecommunicator re-take a test before he or she is terminated? What is the minimum passing score and is the test the same state-wide? Will the law survive a challenge by a veteran dispatcher or a lateral dispatcher from a state without any standards? Change is not easy. Time will tell how successful the new law is.

Chapter Ten: Updating the System

How has 911 changed from the first decade of availability? Does every resident of the United States have access to the three-digit number? What about the funding of 911 with the increased use of cellular telephones verses the traditional hard-lined telephone service? Has the Federal Communications Commission's (FCC) narrow-banding mandate helped or hurt public safety?

Landline phones used to be the standard for residential service. This is no longer true. Some people have both mobile and landline phones while others have moved to the cellular service only. This is problematic for public safety. No longer can a dispatcher answer a 911 call and feel confident that he or she knows where the caller is. Mobile phones have overtaken landlines for personal use.

What are cornerns about VOIP and mobile phones? Location, location, and location! Even when the customer sets their primary address that is no help when the caller is somewhere else. Shall we not forget in a disaster the cellular towers quickly become overwhelmed. The familar message of 'Your caller is not available" is not always due to the person not answering. During times of heavy use, the cellular companies get backed up, hence the calls not going through.

Many call centers have switched to computerized equipment. The old phones and dispatch consoles have gone the way of analog television sets. Computerized equipment is subject bugs and viruses. What happens when the power goes out for an extended time? Most PSAPs have battery backups and generators to manage their critical systems.

The Stratus 2012 Public Safety Survey published these figures when it came to IT Support and Next-Gen 9-1-1:

- 42% of Public Safety Departments have their own data center and IT personnel; 22% have their own data center but outsource IT; 19% use a regional data center

- managed at a central organization; and 9% of PSAPs share the data center with another agency.
- Of those who answered the survey, 34% said their department wasn't instituting NG911 in the next year, 30% said their agency was implementing NG911 and 36% didn't know the status of NG911 technology in their PSAP.
- When asked about running applications in a virtualization environment 62% of the PSAPS have no plans to do so according to the respondents and 35% didn't know one way or the other.
- Technology has improved. 33% of the folks answering the survey reported 2-4 outages, 19% said their agency had one, and 29% had none. A combined 19% made up the rest of the categories.

New 911 Technologies

In the report, *Public Safety Considerations for Smartphone App Developers* by the National Emergency Number Association (NENA) and the Association Public Safety Communications Officials (APCO) published in 2012, next generation 911 is defined as:

"An improved 9-1-1 communication system has been designed based on Internet Protocol (IP), and it is beginning to be implemented in some areas across the United States. It is expected that Canada will follow the transitional pattern soon. This new system, known as Next Generation 9-1-1 (NG911), has the capabilities to support voice, text, video, and additional data. There are many factors (e.g. funding, regulatory) that impact how and when the new NG911 will likely be available on a large scale. In addition, standards developed in the wireless carrier environment may affect the timing of certain types of text support. As a result, NG911 will likely take 8-10 years to evolve across most of the USA and Canada. During this transitional period, while the original legacy E9-1-1 system is still in use, it is imperative that new communications services or technologies that allow users to speak, text, or otherwise communicate with others are able to interoperate with the legacy E9-1-1 and the new NG911 systems in a reliable, seamless manner."

As with any new system upgrade, there are good and bad. Upgrading technology comes with a price, the first concern of any agency. Training of communications center personnel in the use of the NG911 is another. Dispatchers must know how to use the equipment and software associated the NG911. Policies and procedures related to the new data received need to be in place *before* in systems go live. How are texts, pictures, and videos saved? How many are kept and for how long?

Prior to NG911 Public Safety Telecommunicators only heard about the horrific details of crime scenes or traumatic calls. With the new technologies, dispatch personnel may be exposed to live visuals before first responders arrive. Dispatch supervisors should watch for the signs of burn-out or stress in dispatch personnel who have seen graphic images from events where prior to NG911 they would have only had the telephone and/or radio traffic.

One of the key ingredients of NG911 is text-to-911. The advantages of text 911 are obvious. A caller who is deaf or unable to speak, previously utilizing TTY/TDD service or a telephone relay company, is now able to call the public safety agency from anywhere within the department's jurisdiction. People who can't talk due to the circumstances of the incident (in-progress burglary, shooting, hostage, medical, etc.) can text-dial 9-1-1 for help.

In 2012, the Federal Communications Commission announced that all four of the major telecomm companies (AT&T, Verizon, Sprint, and T-Mobile) had agreed to expedite the implementation of text-to-911. The companies agreed to have the service available nationwide by 2014. Just because the telecom industry went along with the FCC doesn't mean the actual service is part of every 911 public safety answering point. Departments still have to acquire the technology and train the communications center personnel.

What happens when a cellular subscriber tries to text 9-1-1 and the carrier does not provide text-to 9-1-1 service? A bounce-

What is Your Emergency? The History of Public Safety Dispatching in America

back message is sent to the caller advising the person to contact the 9-1-1 directly by the traditional method as text-to-9-1-1 is not available in the area.

Currently, most Public Safety Answering Points (PSAPS) do not possess the capability to receive texts, pictures, or videos. For those that can receive the information, as with any call, the Telecommunicator still must verify the information. Whenever possible, direct dialing 9-1-1 is the preferred method of contact for emergency help. The National Emergency Number Association (NENA) has a guideline for agencies with technical information on start-up information (i3 standard).

Voice over Internet Protocol (VoIP) subscribers and many cellular callers can keep phone numbers as they move from one address to another. Many people are not aware that they must manually change their home address in their account to reflect their true physical location for first responders. Stories abound of public safety personnel being dispatched to old locations, and even wrong states, because the victims neglected to update their address with their carrier service. Calls have been received by Public Safety Answering Points from military personnel on cellular phones on base or from off-base locations over-seas for the same reason.

Third party services have sprung up recently claiming to help the public contact 9-1-1. The problem with a third party service is that there is no guarantee of a time frame involved. Is a fee involved (this may be illegible in some states)? In the NENA/APCO report, it is stated "…The app developer should clearly identify how and/or if the caller will be conference to 9-1-1, if necessary. The third party call center's abilities should also be identified (e.g. EMS trained, 9-1-1 center conferencing services provided)."

This isn't your mother's radio system

Visitors walking through the doors of a modern Communications Center would be hard-pressed to recognize which piece of equipment was the radio. Why? With the digital age and

by Diana Sprain

FCC's Narrow-Banding Mandate, many agencies upgraded to computerized radios.

What is re-banding? It began with a Federal Communications Commission mandate that all Public Safety Agencies vacate certain sections of the radio spectrum. The 800 MHz was moved around; this was due in part, to increasing interference from the commercial telecommunications industry and the ever demand for additional opportunities from Public Safety. The deadline for the 700 re-band was set for December 31rst, 2012. Part of this process was the elimination of analog television altogether. Finally, a section of radio called the T-Band (470-512MHz) is slated to be auctioned to the highest commercial bidder in 2023. Any agencies assigned channels within that range will be required to leave the frequencies. The Associated Public Safety Communications Officials (APCO) believes this is unreasonable and is working to get this declaration reversed.

Within Communication Centers, most dispatchers leave the technological aspects of the radios to the techs. Bottom line: does the radio work and will the field units be able to respond back to us? Radios can be integrated with phone systems using touch-screen technology. Some computer-aided dispatching software includes a feature which identifies radios when the microphone is depressed by individual officer. Others may have GPS units installed in field personnel vehicles to better facilitate dispatching.

FirstNet (First Responder Network Authority), or the public safety broadband network, is in development as a means of interoperability communications between agencies using voice, text, and video. When the system is complete, we are promised a complete package in which audio, text, and video data will be live and capable of being shared between responders. FirstNet is one answer to the common problem of agencies being unable to share data relating to incidents but one must remember: FirstNet is not a radio system.

Regional dispatch centers are beginning to replace the 'old-fashioned' local Public Safety Answering Point. This means a radio set-up no longer has just a few channels; instead, depending upon the size of the dispatch center, the screen may have channels

What is Your Emergency? The History of Public Safety Dispatching in America

numbering in the double digits. For larger Communications Centers, this may necessitate splitting up the radio responsibilities to regions (which is supported by most computer-aided dispatch programs as well).

Radio technology is ever-changing. Once the portable radios were bulky pieces of equipment reluctantly carried by firefighters and law enforcement officers; now, portable radios can be small enough to be held within one's hand. The public can tune in and listen live to almost any agency live thanks to the internet. Rather than push a button, a dispatcher touches a screen to select a channel and utilizing a hands-free headset, can move around the communications center to perform records searches while maintaining contact with her field units.

The biggest concern with NG911 and FirstNet is funding. A national coalition was set-up to oversee the 911 infrastructure to NG911. This committee is called NG911 NOW Coalition and consists of representatives from the National Emergency Number Association (NENA), the National Association of State 911 Administrators, and the Industry Council for Emergency Response Technologies (iCERT). A deployment date for nationwide NG911 is 2020. It seems far away but the wireless carriers wanted enough time to convert their systems to IP technology. The FirstNet is supposed to be up and running between 2022-2023.

One barrier is funding: NG911 has been allotted 150 million from the government while FirstNet gets 7 billion. 150 for PSAPS? Well, there had been 43 million available from 2009 to 2012. How much will be allowed for future is still up for consideration. No one is talking about training for the operators. Alas, as dispatchers as well aware: once we complete our initial training we are generally left standing outside lookingin unless we are fortunate enough to work in one of the few states requiring mandatory continuing education.

911 surcharges have been a problem. Allegations of funds being diverted from the 911-specific budget to general funds or reduced charges on wireless not bringing in enough money to pay for the upgrades are hampering the efforts. States also tend to divert money to firefighting or law enforcement over

communications. To help stop the bleeding, Congress placed a stipulation that any 911 organization wishing money to upgrade to NG911 must certify that 180 days from the date of their application no money has been diverted from the 911 accounts for any other purpose.

In an article published in Emergency Management, Patrick Halley, the executive director of the NG911 Institute is quoted as saying "...The FCC has studied how much each state collects in 911 fees and sought to determine the percentages each was spending in components of an NG911 system, and nationwide the average is less than 10 percent...the 911 basically works today. There are no wide-scale failures. That fact may lower the sense of urgency on the part of policy-makers. But the PSAPs' capabilities are completely limited to what they could be, and as infrastructure providers sunset their lehacy networks, it is going to be 911 systems that are out on an island. So I don't think policymakers feel that urgency to say we need to start moving forward now."

What happened to my dispatch console?

Long or u-shaped desks with two or three monitors; a time clock to stamp the call and status cards; the belt which brings up new cards and sends back completed ones; numerous maps of the response areas with beats & districts drawn out; and a bookcase of references. That was the dispatch console of the old-school Public Safety Dispatcher. As each event was initiated, units dispatched, and the incident completed, dispatchers would time stamp the record. The console had what seemed to be an endless series of multi-colored buttons: buttons for radios, intercoms, alarms, alert tones, and door unlocks. Dispatchers ruled the department from their consoles. Those without computers or cards used logs. It was awkward, but it worked. A majority of departments have since converted to the electronic age. Computer-aided dispatch software replaced the outdate card or log system. The card carrying be

The modern console, or workstation has multiple monitors to accommodate the computerized telephone & radio systems, ring-down (paging) for fire and emergency medical services, email, in-

What is Your Emergency? The History of Public Safety Dispatching in America

house data systems, and computer-aided dispatch (CAD) software. If a department handles law enforcement, the dispatchers need access to the FBI's NCIC, as well as their state and/or local data systems. Internal data bases or references are also commonly used.

New public safety answering points are being designed with dispatchers in mind. Consoles have individully controlled lights. Ergonomics are important: keyboards pull out and tilt. Vendors offer workstations that raise up, allowing the dispatcher to stand or sit at will as they work. Headsets are lightweight and can be the traditional corded or hands-free with a push-to-talk option. Maps are integrated to the CAD system.

Vendors customize consoles to individual department's specifications. Whether one wants the paging hardware installed in the console equipment or just wants the basic radio (provided the department isn't using a touch-screen or IP-based radio system), it is all negotiable. Design should make the most of the space in the best ergonomic design to assist the dispatcher in the performance of his or her job.

Dispatcher health has become a concern. One agency made news when it installed treadmills inside the communications center. Dispatchers are at risk for cardiovascular disease, diabetes, and other medical problems due to the nature of the job. It is up to us to change our lifestyles.

Chapter Eleven: Major Incidents and Disasters

Major incidents and disasters can happen anytime. Ask any Telecommunicator who has worked critical incidents and he or she will tell you no one called ahead with a warning about the Loma Prieta earthquake or the San Bruno Explosion. Even when weather forecasters gave advance notice of Hurricane Sandy, the event still impacted the region's resources for months after the winds stopped and waters receded.

Communications Center and Disaster Operations Managers must have a contingency place for a back-up Dispatch Center in case the primary Public Safety Answering Point (PSAP) is rendered unusable or destroyed. During an extended event, Public Safety Telecommunicators may work alternate schedules, with days off & vacations cancelled. Dispatchers need immediate, secured, access to bathroom, showers, a sleeping area, a quiet room, lockers, and a kitchen with a refrigerator and a microwave.

We're Taking Rocks & Bottles: Demonstrations and Riots

In 1996 St. Petersburg, Florida experienced a series of riots as a result of an officer-involved shooting. The dispatch center was specifically mentioned in the United Stated Fire Administration's Technical Report series (via the after action report). In the eight page section, the review of dispatch's role was thoroughly broken down. During the review period, the 911 calls were sent to a mobile command post staffed by fire personnel via a pager system and then closed out. The Computer-Aided Dispatch (CAD) system was temporarily set-up via a grid system to alert dispatchers of the involved area. They did their best to track duplicate calls, but as they closed out calls after sending each one to the Incident Command Post (ICP), some redundant calls managed to get sent regardless. Reading the report, it is clear that a certain amount of bitterness was present by not allowing the very folks who man the radios & telephones on a daily basis to handle the job during the crisis at the Incident Command Post.

What is Your Emergency? The History of Public Safety Dispatching in America

On March 3, 1991, the infamous beating of Rodney King by members of the Los Angeles Police Department occurred. Mr. King was originally stopped by an officer for a traffic violation, after he refused to pull over. At the time, Rodney King was on parole for a robbery offense. Unbeknownst to the officers, they were recorded as they proceeded to beat the man. Around the same time, a Korean store owner shot and killed a young black woman accused of stealing a beverage. The two situations were a powder keg waiting to explode.

The LAPD officers were found not guilty and the Korean store owner only received probation and a fine. Outrage from both sentences torched a riot in South Central Los Angeles that lasted six days. Riots also broke out in other cities across the nation, including Las Vegas, Oakland, Berkeley, Seattle, Chicago, and San Francisco; in all, 25 people died and over one billion dollars in damages were tallied. King himself went on television, where he made his famous speech saying, "Can't we all just get along?"

Some cities are magnets for demonstrations or riots while others are fortunate to have never seen one at all. In July 1999 the public broadcast news radio, station KPFA, in the City of Berkeley announced it was changing its format. The radio staff expected some anger: what they received was far greater than they could have imagined: ten steady days of protests and off & on again demonstrations through August of 1999. Thanks to the internet, print news, and the television, people arrived from all areas of the USA to join the fight to save KPFA radio. The City of Berkeley was inundated with thousands of people holding up signs, marching in the streets, and causing mayhem. One rally alone drew an estimated crowd of up to 15,000 people, who walked through the streets. The protest ended on the University of Berkeley campus.

Before any crowd gathers for a protest or a spark ignites a riot, every dispatcher should find, read, and understand the agency's policy and procedure for a response to a demonstration and/or riot. How does the agency handle said incident? Most law enforcement agencies should have a basic protocol for a demonstration and/or riot call, but what of fire or emergency medical services? Does the fire or ems dispatch have one for that type of call? Does the Communications Center handle the call from Dispatch, or is the event run from a secondary place (an Incident Command Post or back-up emergency operations center)? If the agency has Tactical Dispatchers or Incident Dispatch Team, do those personnel take over the event? Never assume you can look up how to deal with this type of response when it happens, for it will be too late and you will be too busy then.

I Need Help!

Nothing stops a dispatcher's heart beating like a distress call over a radio. A field person requesting emergency help trumps all other incidents handled by radio dispatchers. Unlike those calls involving the public, mass casualties, disasters, or the weird events, these events involve our own. If the first responders are down & out, they can't help the public. Even more so, many times, we (the dispatchers) *know* the man or woman calling on the radio. We've been to their home for a BBQ, babysat their kids, or it's one of our family members. As much as we try to remain unbiased and professional, a part of us can't help but become personally involved.

The world stops until that unit is located and the suspect is caught or the firefighter/emergency medical personnel are rescued. In the last decade there have been numerous terrible events including too many in which multiple officers were shot over different parts of the country in a single incident. Whether the law enforcement agency suffers one down or many, the impact is still the same. Everyone involved in the event feels the loss and responsibility. Fire department maydays or ems calls for help or no less stressful or important.

One of the more infamous events in modern law enforcement history is the North Hollywood (CA) Bank of America Robbery, which occurred on February 28th, 1997. The two suspects entered the financial institution just after the bank opened and demanded money, emphasizing their request with shots fired with their AK-47 and M-16 assault rifles. Exiting the bank, the robbers were immediately confronted by members of the Los Angeles Police Department. A forty minute fire-fight ensued between the two suspects covered in body armor and the police. The ever helpful media was quickly on scene, filming the incident live.

The Los Angeles Police Communications Unit is located in downtown LA. The on-duty Radio Telephone Operators (RTO) for the North Hollywood division that morning were Police Service Representative (PSR) Joanna Ramirez, Robyn Frazier, Tonja Bellard, Karen Koukal, Deborah Clayton, and Guadalupe de la Cruz. Guadalupe had just taken over the radio to give the dispatcher on the North Hollywood channel a break. In an interview for an article in 9-1-1 Magazine, de la Cruz said,

"9L89 reported he was enroute to the bank. 9L89 is a one-man unit. It was just seconds later that he came in yelling, 'Live shots fired!" And I could hear the shots in the background. SO I immediately put out the information he gave me, and after that, he started screaming for help, because he'd been shot."

Frazier added, "One injured officer, Stuart Guy, just stopped broadcasting. He felt that he was going to be all right, since the suspects moved past him, but because they kept spraying bullets, no one could approach him. When he stopped broadcasting, we almost forgot that he still needed someone to go to him."

On that day, there were a total of seven civilians, one dog, and eleven Los Angeles police officers wounded. Over 1100 rounds were discharged by the suspects. The Communications Center was inundated by 911 telephone calls as the incident escalated. The radio traffic increased well beyond the normal to the point where the dispatch staff abandoned the computer-aided dispatch system and resorted to paper notes. Once the incident was over, the dispatch staff was honored by the Department for their actions on that infamous day.

A different officer down event happened in the north part of the state involving officers of the Oakland (CA) Police department in 2009. On Saturday at 1:00 p.m, two Oakland motor units, a sergeant and an officer, made a car stop on MacArthur Blvd in the east end of the city. After calling in the location, the two officers approached the vehicle only to be shot multiple times by the driver.

by Diana Sprain

The shooter exited his vehicle and shot the officers one more time and then he fled the scene. A call for help came in by members of the public via 911, prompting a massive response of 115 units after the 'Officer Needs Help' was broadcast. The Oakland Police found an identification card in the vehicle left at the crime scene. Two more officers and the suspect were killed during the forced entry and confrontation. The radio dispatcher handling the incident was assisted by her co-workers, as would any telecommunicator in the same situation, allowing her to keep cool during the entire event.

Officer involved shooting incidents are high profile events and the personnel rely on dispatch personnel to keep calm, even if field personnel are screaming over the radio. Public Safety Telecommunicators must be able to direct the activity and track units at all times. Veteran dispatchers may get to the point where they can recognize an individual unit just by voice alone; which doesn't excuse field personnel from identifying themselves via a proper call-sign but in a true emergency, this ability can reduce time and save a life in this type of incident.

Fire and emergency medical personnel aren't exempt from distress calls. In previous chapters, incidents involving firefighters needing emergency assistance at wildland fires were reviewed. When a fire breaks out in a structure, the Incident Commander must keep track of the firefighters but Communications Center Telecommunicators should pay attention to the radio for critical status updates or calls for help and ensure that information is relayed to the Incident Commander. Many after-action reports cite distress calls overlooked due to the radio channels overwhelmed with conversations or dispatchers unfamiliar with the fire ground terminology. Another problem occurs when the dispatchers are unable to understand what firefighters are saying as the voices are muffled when speaking with their face masks on.

Emergency Medical personnel can find themselves in dicey situations at any time. One paramedic was treating an assault victim when the man suddenly pulled out a gun and pointed the weapon at the officer on scene. In response, the officer drew down on the injured man. The poor paramedic was caught between the stand-off. In inner cities and urban areas, EMTs and paramedics

What is Your Emergency? The History of Public Safety Dispatching in America

might wear body armor to protect themselves. Many crews have called dispatch to report a person shooting at their ambulance (the reflective Star of Life can be a target). Disgruntled citizens have set fires or called in medical problems, only to shoot at the first responders or ambulance crews in an ambush attack.

Dispatchers should review their Department policies and procedures in advance of an incident. Listen to audio tapes of incidents to understand the types of radio traffic one can expect for these types of call.

When taking traffic stops or contacts, know which field unit you are taking the information from. Following Department protocol, always confirm the location if you are uncertain what the unit told you. NEVER tell a field unit calling in a stop to stand by UNLESS another one is calling in a call for help. That one time may be his or her only opportunity to provide you with the location. For those who dispatch units in rural locations where response from cover units can take hours, this is even more important.

One major difference between standard street cops and rural law enforcement by an agency such as Nevada Department of Wildlife is the type of terrain involved for patrolling. Fish & Game Wardens enforce wildlife, hunting, fishing, and boating laws of the state they work for. As legally authorized law enforcement personnel, warden can come across any type of criminal activity, medical emergencies, and fires. A Fish & Game officer must be prepared to handle just about anything. In many cases, their patrols take them in areas where cover (back-up) is hours away. The terrain may be accessible by four-wheel drive, ATV, helicopter, horseback, or foot. A good portion of the subjects contacted by game wardens carry guns as they are hunters. Game wardens might be on a boat performing water patrol. This doesn't prevent them from finding trouble. A person driving a boat under the influence is just as guilty of a crime as the person driving a car under the influence. They might come across a person wanted on a warrant or stumble on a pot field that is booby-trapped. Game wardens get into pursuits, foot chases, have to break up fights, or look for missing persons just like a street cop in addition to investigating poaching cases or dealing with a troublesome bear.

Alas, law enforcement has come under attack in recent years. False calls for assistance have been made to lure in officers, who are then targeted by shooters. Fire and emergency service personnel are not exempt from the anger. One man started a fire and when the fire department arrived, began shooting at the field personnel. He continued to fire when law enforcement arrived on scene.

Active Shooter Incidents

Have active shooter incidents become more prevalent or has the media just covered more of the stories? Has the 24 hour availability of the Internet made a difference in the frequency of these incidents whereas the pre-Internet media limited the coverage of the events and thus possibly kept said calls from occurring?

Active shooter calls have happened since the invention of guns. One of the worst incidents (until Orlando) terms of lives lost was the Virginia Polytechnic Institute and State University shooting, which took place on 16th of April, 2007. The responsible shooter killed 32 students & faculty members and wounded another 17 before committing suicide. Virginia Tech Police Department (VTPD) dispatch's normal call volume jumped from an average of 400 to 500 calls to over 2,000 in a day. The radio traffic also escalated as the incident progressed. The usual university police staff is 2 dispatchers and one supervisor, but that morning staffing had been adjusted to allow leave usage for the day. One dispatcher was on duty pending late arrival of the other staff. The single dispatcher called office personnel to help with phones until the other dispatcher and supervisor arrived. After the communications center had full staffing, the radio and phones were split, instead of shared as per the normal VTPD procedure.

The Columbine High School shooting which occurred on the 20th day of April in 1999 was a shocker because the suspects were two students. Public Safety Telecommunicators received multiple 9-1-1 calls from the school staff and student and a fire alarm.

What is Your Emergency? The History of Public Safety Dispatching in America

Columbine High had a School Resource Officer present at the time and he did confront the suspects, with reported gunfire exchanged between them. We know now that the suspects had brought various hi-power and automatic weapons, along with almost 100 incendiary or explosive devices, planning on an extended terrorist-style attack. During the active search for the suspects and rescue operations for victims, public safety personnel came across the improvised incendiary & explosive devises. At the end of the incident, First Responders found 13 dead and treated over 160 for injuries (24 were seriously wounded). To date, the worst incident on record is the Orlando (FL) nightclub incident inwhich 49 people were killed and 50 wounded on the 12th of June, 2016.

Other recent mass shootings include Sandy Hook Elementary and Aurora Movie Theatre. The theater shooting was made more heinous when the shooter booby-trapped his apartment with explosives. Older events include the McDonalds shooting in San Diego and Texas Tower Sniper (the Watch Tower). The Associated Public Safety Communications Officials (APCO) along with many private training companies has courses available for active shooters. The Department of Homeland Security (DHS) has a free on-line class (at the time of this writing) with the basic steps to take if one is involved in such an event.

Keeping calm and tracking all field personnel is important. Following the departments' policy & procedure in reference to this type of incident is also important – as is reading the documentation *prior* to the need for its use.

Send Everything You Have: Mass Casualty Incidents

Major events where injuries can total in the triple digits quickly overwhelm resources. The Cocoanut Grove was a popular entertainment club in Boston (MA). Ignoring safety recommendations, the exit doors were secured. A fire broke out and quickly spread on the 28th of November, 1942. The crowd panicked, resulting in a pile of bodies at the doors and 492 people dead. In 1944 a fire in the main tent of the Ringling Brothers Circus on 6th of July, 1944 in Hartford (CT) left 167 people dead and 500 injured. The St. Francis Dam at Santa Clarita (CA) failed in 1928, its deadly flood waters killed 600 people. The MGM Grand Hotel in Las Vegas (NV) on November 21, 1980 caught fire and left 84 dead. In 1981, the Kansas City (KS) Hyatt Regency Hotel's new skywalks collapsed, killing 114. More recent incidents include a train derailment at Lac-Megantic, Canada which killed 47 and destroyed a large portion of the town; the Boston Marathon bombing which killed two but injured 264; an airplane crash at the 2011 Reno Air Races left 11 killed and 70 injured; and the 1980 Mount St. Helens eruption killed 57 people and devastated the region.

Each of these events not only stretched the field resources, but taxed the communications center personnel to their limits. As these events happened, the rest of the agency's jurisdiction didn't stop the everyday activities: folks still became ill, other fires broke out, and crimes occurred. Dispatch personnel had to juggle calls for service, determining which calls had priority over those which could wait until additional resources arrived to help. Before TET teams, dispatch had to rely on their own to staff dispatch in the worst situations. Until help arrives, dispatchers have to make the tought decisions on managing the event, and the rest of the calls coming in. People don't stop getting sick or needing help just because a major incident is in progress.

In mass casualty incidents, the initial estimates of victims may be inaccurate. First Responders, unable to make contact with dispatch due to the unusual amount of radio traffic and busy phone lines, may self-dispatch to the scene. In a recent school shooting in Sparks (NV), over 150 field personnel arrived to assist. How many of those units self dispatched? That leads to another question…with no one coordinating the response of field personnel, who is covering the rest of the city and/or county? A person must be declared in charge, hence the use of the Incident Command System (ICS) or the National Incident Management System (NIMS). Any requests should go through the Incident Commander and documented in the call log. Radio control must be kept, even sending the incident to another channel or breaking up the event to multiple channels if possible (have Incident

Commander make decision or if that is not realistic, keep dispatch on one, event on two, medical on three, etc.).

"Part of the Bridge Collapsed" – Earthquakes

Most people think of California as earthquake central, and granted the majority of our countries larger quakes tend to be in the west coast with the largest loss of lives to date being the 1906 San Francisco earthquake (and fire) in which up to 6,000 persons perished. During the 1971 Sylmar (CA) earthquake, the Veteran's Hospital and Olive View Medical Center Hospital both suffered major damage during the 6.6 Richter scale shaking.

In 1989, the Loma Prieta (CA) quake shook hard enough to dislodge a small upper section of the Oakland-Bay Bridge, sending it crashing down to the lower section. The Cypress Structure, which connected traffic from I-580/80 to Highway 17 (now called 880), completed collapsed when the upper section pan-caked on top of the lower part. In San Francisco, in the Marina District, fires broke out in quake-damaged buildings. Across the Bay, in Berkeley, a general alarm fire stretched the City's resources while the fire department also handled the many other calls for quake-related calls. That day the San Francisco Bay Area was fortunate in that the World Series was scheduled to start at 5:00 P.M.; many left work early that afternoon – a choice that most likely saved their lives. Calls quickly exceeded resources and until help was able to come in from outside the region, dispatchers had no choice but to let calls accumulate, sending units to the highest priority and then down the list as resources became available (this is referred to as 'stacking').

Stacking calls for fire or emergency medical services is only done in the worst conditions. A dispatcher will advise the field supervisor of any new calls, who makes the determination on which calls are handled in which order according to the problem. Once the conditions improve, service goes back to normal dispatch order.

Other states also have had earthquakes. Alaska was devastated by an earthquake and a tsunami that killed 165 people in 1946.

by Diana Sprain

Washington, D.C. is still completing repairs from a trembler: no one was killed but the shaker disrupted the government and did serious damage to many buildings. Recent severe quakes in Japan, Haiti, and Nepal resulted in massive devastation. The Japan quake triggered a tsunami to complicated matters. The loss of life and damages was astronomical.

Earthquakes are long-term events. Aftershocks can occur for weeks or months later, causing further damage to buildings and roadways. The number one rule in dealing with earthquakes is to make sure the first responders (including dispatchers) are okay first. Does your agency have a policy & procedure on earthquakes? If not, do a general roll-call for every person you know is on duty. Tone the fire and emergency medical stations. Ask for injury and damage reports – let the watch commander, ems supervisor, and battalion chief know the status of the field personnel & equipment. Only once you know what you have to work with in terms of personnel and equipment can you help the public.

Major Wildland Fires

In 1991, the Oakland-Berkeley firestorm began after a fire from the previous day rekindled during the perfect red flag conditions. 25 people, including one firefighter and one police officer, died and over 3,354 structures were destroyed. The total loss added up to 1.5 billion dollars. In October of 2007, the hot and dry weather started ignited a series of wildfires in the San Diego area of California, which required over one million people to evacuate their homes. When the flames were finally doused, 23 large fires were tallied, 3000 structures destroyed, and fourteen people were killed as a result of the conflagrations. The rough acreage burned was about 518,021. In 2013, a series of wildfires in the Western states in general taxed the resources of the USFS and BLM. In June of 2013, 19 firefighters were killed in Yarnell, Arizona fighting the Yarnell Hill blaze.

Wildland fires can last days or weeks. Smoke from the flames drift according to the prevailing winds, dropping ash over a wide area causing unhealthy conditions for residents. Flames travel where fuel and wind dictate, and again, conditions can change in a moment's notice requiring evacuations but not all people are willing to leave their property. In addition to residents, Public Safety must contend with livestock, companion animals, and wildlife displaced by the spreading fire. Panicked animals can be a road hazard to responding crews. Downed power lines are another hazard dispatchers should keep in mind.

Hurricanes/Tornadoes

Hurricanes and tornadoes are unique in that they occur every year but not in the same place. Technology has improved over the years allowing weather forecasters to predict hurricane paths, which allow those living in the projected areas to prepare for the storms. The tornadoes are not as reliable, sometimes touching ground with little warning. Both weather events can devastate an area in a very short amount of time.

The worst hurricane in 'modern' United States history occurred in 1900: the Galveston (TX) hurricane hit the City hard, killing an estimated 6,000 to 12,000 people. Katrina hit shores in 2005, taking 1,836 and causing an estimated 108 billion damages in damages. A tornado that swept through Joplin (MO) in May of 2011 killed 158, destroying the town. A 1953 tornado that touched down in Waco (TX) left 114 dead. Hurricane Sandy hit in 2012, with 68 billion dollars in damages and 283 people killed. Countless others were displaced by the storm.

The problem with hurricanes is the associated storm surges, heavy rain, and high winds. The bad weather that arrives before the actual storm creates hazards for people trying to leave the area. Residents who decide to 'ride out the storm' may get in trouble and need rescue when they become trapped.

First responders have to negotiate debris, downed power lines, and environmental hazards in order to help those in need. In some cases, public safety personnel, their equipment, and their facilities may be directly impacted by the hurricane. Critical services (phones, electricity, water, gas) may be knocked out for an extended amount of time. Cell towers can be impacted either by damage or by over-whelmed switches, leaving areas normally relying on mutual aid on their own until mutual aid from agencies outside the strike zone can arrive.

Erik Auf der Heide in his book writing about the Waco tornado in his book *Disaster Response* noted, "The tornado struck at 4.40 p.m. but coordination did not even begin to emerge until a meeting at state police headquarters at 11:30 p.m. 'We finally organized a disaster committee, with the power to make the decisions and…pass final judgment on any particular question…"

Storing supplies in a storm cellar as disaster books suggest for the communications center is a good idea. Have a couple of dispatchers licensed as mobile HAM radio operators, with a working radio within dispatch. HAM radio consistently worked during the disaster when all other communications systems failed or were grossly overwhelmed. Another last ditch option to keep in dispatch is an old-fashioned CB radio. When nothing else works, the cb radio usually will.

Other Weather Events

In 1980 the county was fighting a major heat wave. When the weather pattern finally broke, an estimated 1,700 people had died from the effects of the heat. The Ohio River flooded in 1937, killing 380 people and causing 5 billion dollars in damages. In 1960, a tsunami struck Hawaii and Alaska after an earthquake hit Chile; the deadly waves were responsible for killing 61 lives on the island. A 1999 heat wave took over 250 lives. A blizzard that blanketed the eastern portion of the United States resulted in an estimated 353 deaths.

In June of 2012, a derecho caused a number of 911 Public Safety Answering Points (PSAPs) and wireless networks to fail. A derecho is defined as "a massive windstorm that results from a fast-moving line of thunderstorms". The effects of the 2012 storm lasted over multiple days, preventing residents from calling emergency personnel via 911 due to the circuits being out of service. The area reached from Washington to Chicago. The FCC later fined the phone companies involved for their role in the failure.

Aircraft Crashes

The worst single aircraft accident within the United States to date happened in 1978 in Chicago (IL), when American Airlines Flight went down with 273 on board. TWA Flight 800 went down with 230 on board in 1996. Another flight, PSA 182, crashed in a residential neighborhood in San Diego. The results were unlike anything the US had seen before. The commercial airliner collided with a small Cessna over the skies of San Diego (CA). The commercial passenger jet took out multiple city blocks when it hit the ground. Forward to July of 2013, to San Francisco (CA) International Airport, the scene of the most recent aircraft incident: Asiana Airlines which caught its tail upon landing, flipped around and killed three and injured 200. We've also seen planes land in the Hudson River (NY) with a 100% survival rate.

A more likely scenario for an average dispatcher is a hard landing of a helicopter or a crash of a small private plane or a commercial plane reporting a problem with the landing gear requiring an activation of a county protocol. Again, knowing what to do ahead of time is critical, especially for fire or emergency medical dispatchers. Where are the stand-by points, the triage areas, and which personnel are to be notified? Understanding the procedures, or at least knowing where the call-out list is kept, in advance of an actual incident will make a difference when seconds truly count.

9-11: The Day the Towers Fell

One of the worst days in public safety occurred when our country was attacked without provocation. Once the fires were out, the death toll was calculated to be just under 3,000 with countless others injured. Four aircraft were hijacked to used as weapons of mass destructions – three successfully and one denied by a group of brave passengers. First responders and civilians were both lost in the towers trying to rescue victims and put out fires.

During the craziness of the attacks, the dispatchers had to contend with panicked victims, witnesses, family members, and field personnel all wanting help, directions, and information in a situation no one could ever comprehend such an incident would occur. Radio channels were quickly overwhelmed with incoming and outgoing transmissions. Because many police, fire, and ems units self-dispatched, tracking personnel was very challenging. Due to issues with radio signals within the buildings, some messages weren't received. Regardless, the communications staff did a fantastic job under the worst circumstances. When the towers started falling, the confusion only became worse. How does one train for such an event, much less an incident in which a significant portion of your units suddenly are gone?

The Bottom Line: What have we learned about major events?

Time after time the after-action reports come down to a couple of similar problems: the lack of radio interoperability between multiple agencies and communications problems with dispatch centers. In response to the radio interoperability the Federal Communications Center (FCC) came up with FirstNet. This broadband frequency is the promised network that all first responders will be able to use in the future, regardless of which service (law, fire, or emergency medical services). Just think: live video and audio feeds available to first responders. Will it work? Let us hope so.

Communications Centers must be trained in the Incident Command System (ICS) and the National Incident Management System (NIMS). Both ICS and NIMS utilize standard procedures and terminology. Each system can be used for a simple call and are designed to grow with the event as needed. The Incident Command System has been slightly modified to be used by law enforcement and hospitals. There is no reason for any Public Safety Telecommunicator NOT to learn and use the program, especially

What is Your Emergency? The History of Public Safety Dispatching in America

as the training is offered for free as a 'learn at your own pace' on-line by the Federal Emergency Management Agency (FEMA). Communications Center Managers can download the training and provide the course on paper to their dispatch personnel if that is the better option.

A good article on the Incident Command System for dispatchers is available on the 9-1-1 Magazine website. Look up *Dispatch ICS* by Randall Larson, written on December 8, 2011.

Dispatchers should disregard all radio codes and use plain talk (no radio codes) when relaying requests to other Public Safety Answering Points, hospitals, government agencies, or private companies. Dr. Eric Auf der Heide wrote in his book, *Disaster Response: Principles of Preparation and Coordination:* "The effectiveness of disaster response may depend on the ability of organizations to share resources. However, when requesting resources from another organization, the lack of standardized terminology may make it difficult to know what one may receive. The ability of a requested fire truck to carry out the mission for what it is requested may depend on the equipment it carries, its water capacity, and the number and training of its crew. All of these factors may vary among the different fire departments."

One method to discover any kinks in the system ahead of a real disaster is by holding annual disaster drills. Many agencies hold drills, both actual and table-top. The table-top drills are done in an office environment, where no personnel are physically activated as compared to an actual drill utilizing volunteers and public safety personnel. To make a drill as realistic as possible, the planners should not announce the drill in advance, only notifying the volunteers. This will allow a true measure of the public safety system response. After the event is completed, all involved personnel should be invited to the debriefing to discussed what went well and what needs to be improved.

A few years back I was dispatching for an agency that held a disaster drill. A person was sent to the communications center to act as an assistant due to the increased amount of phones and radio traffic. The Incident Commander didn't think to ask if I wanted or needed help, or what type of help would be appropriate. The woman was willing but she couldn't answer the phones or the radio. She had no idea what to do and I sent her back to the emergency operations center. My supervisor showed up wanting to know why I released the woman. She was more of a hindrance than help. It was easier to deal with the event (and my real work) by myself than continually tell her what to do. That just tripled my workload. Alas, I didn't get to attend the debriefing to pass this on. Only 'admin' was allowed at the meeting. What is the purpose of having a drill if only the chiefs get to discuss how it went? They pat themselves on the back and move on. Meanwhile, when the real emergency hits who actually handles the event in the initial stages? The ones who were locked out from the debriefing: the worker bees.

During disasters, dispatchers may be asked to deal with problems they have never dealt with in their career. Which agency do they contact do clear the air of nuisance helicopters? Who can they call to request tractors needed for rescue operations in the middle of the night? Who can get a refrigeration truck to store bodies in the middle of August at the spur of the moment in a rural area? Where do you get fifty additional portable radios? What happens when dispatch is damaged and there is no back-up center? Understand that the public will call asking for directions on what to do. The media will call wanting updates about the situation. Until the agency public information person arrives, dispatch will be the contact. After the Loma Prieta earthquake stopped its initial shaking, many of us had to delay our response until the bridges were inspected and declared safe (the Bay area relies on bridges to cross the many waterways). During the KPFA riots, we had to show ID to get in the building. During one wildfire near where I lived, I was on eggshells hoping the wind changed. How could I go to work when I was worried about possibly evacuating? This is a valid concern for any agency dealing with a disaster. Personnel must be able to secure their families.

In the post 9-11 days, the most common drills have switched from aircraft-related events to terrorist incidents but are we really planning for the most likely incidents? Public Safety Managers should take a serious look at their areas and consider what events

What is Your Emergency? The History of Public Safety Dispatching in America

have the highest chance of occurring. For example: in May of 1991 the City of Henderson dealt with a liquefied gas leak requiring a massive evacuation of people. The resulting cloud sent over 200 people to local hospital emergency rooms and left 30 admitted. Communications was an issue, as with most of the major incidents, the lack of interoperability between agencies was a problem. The other issue was a compromised cellular telephone system. Any department which relies on cellular telephones may be in for a surprise when calls are directed to voicemail.

After 9-11, Clark County disaster drills switched focus from aircraft crashes to terrorist attacks yet a little known incident occurred on August 7, 2007, when a railroad car containing liquefied chlorine rolled away and travelled a significant distance through Las Vegas before officials managed to stop it.

It helps to play the 'what if' game during some quiet time and see if the answers to odd questions are available. If not, seek the information. Waiting for a major incident is too late.

When a major incident occurs that requires both joint fire and law enforcement resources, the commanders for each side should work together for a stream-lined approach to manage the event. The Unified Command, another feature of Incident Command System, is an excellent way to handle an in-progress call of any size. Unified Command allows for police, fire, and emergency medical services to manage the event from start to finish, whether it stays at a small local size or grows to a Federal level.

One lesson learned by prior events is that the cellular phone system becomes unusable due to the excessive volume of calls initiated. Landline phones may also become overwhelmed. Old fashioned citizen's band (CB) radios may be a viable option for communications. The one stand-out option is the HAM radio operators. HAM radios work when most other technological components fail. If possible, arranging for some dispatch personnel to get certified and licensed as HAM operators and then to install a HAM radio in an accessible place, such as the emergency Operations Center, would be a great back-up in the event of a disaster.

Chapter Twelve: Doing the Job

The dispatcher lifestyle: shift work

During oral board interviews and probably somewhere on the written test, a question is posed to all telecommunicator candidates: can you work evenings, nights, weekends, holidays or overtime? Of course, most everyone answers yes. In fact, twenty five years, I only had one person tell me no: she didn't get past the oral board.

Any 911 Public Safety Answering Point (PSAP) is staffed twenty-four hours a day /seven-day a week. We also refer to this type of dispatch as a 24/7 – or a traditional PSAP. Traditional PSAPs handle law enforcement, and may also handle the city (or county) fire, emergency medical services, animal control, public works, or parking enforcement. In some areas, multiple cities can join together with the county for a regional center. Departments may contract to other local, state, or federal departments to provide dispatching services.

Another type of communications center, also a 24/7, is a secondary Public Safety Answering Point. This center is separate from the law enforcement and typically manages fire services. In many secondary PSAPs, the Emergency Medical Services may also be dispatched from this center or it, too, may have its own dispatch. Finally there is a third communications center type: the non-traditional PSAP. Non-traditional communications centers may not receive 911 calls directly (but the callers can be transferred to the dispatchers). These communication centers may have limited staffing hours or seasonal hours. The agency I work for is open from six am to eleven pm seven days a week. We do ocasionally modify our hours depedning on need from field personnel and we're closed for Christmas and Thanskgiving.

Alternate Public Safety Answering Points or non-traditional centers can handle law enforcement, fire, or emergency medical services. Telecommunicators still perform the same duties as their counterparts in traditional PSAPs, minus the 9-1-1 calls. Does that mean those dispatchers don't receive emergency calls? Absolutely

What is Your Emergency? The History of Public Safety Dispatching in America

not: in fact, many of the Telecommunicators handle panicked callers reporting fights, medical emergencies, boat accidents, fires, and animal-related events on the direct-dial numbers or tip hotlines. Poaching calls in progress, shooting incidents, brush fires, and search & rescue calls come in at all hours.

Actual shifts vary according to the department but the common ones are an eight hour shift five days a week (5/8); ten hour shifts four days a week (4/10); and a varying twelve hour shift. From my survey, dispatchers wrote about working two eight hour shifts one week and two twelve hours the next week, working the same twenty-four hour shift as the firefighters (a ten-day day a month schedule) and working part-time.

Time off (vacation, sick leave) also varies according to individual departments, as do benefits. The vacation sign-ups are as varied as the shifts. From personal experience, I have been required to put in for vacation a year in advance, a couple of months ahead of time, and a few weeks in advance. Selecting a shift, whether one has seniority or not, can be as much as a crapshoot as a day in a Vegas casino. One agency did a shift bid quarterly strictly according to seniority: climb the totem pole and one could stay on a shift, with chosen days off as long as you wanted to. Another department I worked for plugged each new employee in to a slot, which had a mandatory rotation. Each quarter everyone rotated from days to swings to nights, switching days off as well. You knew what you would be working a year at a time, but there was no choice in the rotation. At my current department, we bid when an employee is hired and completes training and unless we convince the supervisor to make a new schedule for re-bid, the shift & days off is *it*. Am I for a 'permanent' shift verses a chance to rotate? I can see the benefits in both.

In October of 2012, Status Technologies released a report based upon a survey conducted in the Public Safety field. The questions focused on the Public Safety Answering Points (PSAP) and the dispatchers, but the company did receive responses from First Responders. Among some of the statistics included in the report were:

- 39% of the people answering the survey were Communications Center Managers, 10% were First Responders, and 9% were primarily Dispatchers
- Most of the respondents worked for a County (48%) with the next largest group being employed by a City or Town (35%). My employer group (State) came in at 4%
- The jurisdictional population average size was less than 80,000 (53%); mid-level size of 80,000 to 200,000 came in with 25% and jurisdictions over 200,000 had a 20% response.
- Call volume depends on population (makes sense- more people make more calls but not every 9-1-1 call requires a dispatch.)
- 74% of call-taking and radio dispatch are handled separately.

Passing it on: becoming a trainer

How much time passes before one is qualified or suitable to become a trainer? I took my first trainee a year after starting at Berkeley. I have lost count of how many men and woman have sat next to me over the years. Most passed although there were a few who didn't have the skills necessary to perform the job. Teaching another person is difficult and not everyone has the patience or ability to be an instructor. I was sent to a school where I was certified as a Civilian-Training Officer. I enjoy showing a new person the ropes. Sure, it's work but in the end I know I'm working with a man or woman who understands the job.

After a suitable time period passes a Public Safety Telecommunicator may be asked to mentor, or train, a new hire. For those fortunate folks, this may mean first attending a Civilian Training Officer (CTO) course first. CTO courses are available through private training companies, the Associated Public Safety Communications Officials, Inc. (APCO), many state's Peace

What is Your Emergency? The History of Public Safety Dispatching in America

Officers Standard and Training (POST), and a few local community colleges.

Formal training as a Civilian Training Officer *should be* required before accepting a trainee. A Civilian Training Officer class does more than show a dispatcher how to pass on knowledge. Liability, legal issues, evaluation techniques, and methods of imparting knowledge are reviewed in the class. Consider this: no fire department or law enforcement agency allows an officer or firefighter, fresh from the academy to go out and start running calls; nor does that department put that new person with the most junior field person without any training experience (and without a Field Training Officer certification). Why? The combination is a pending train wreck with a crowd of lawyers lined up, pending lawsuit paperwork in hand. So why do Communications Managers, Supervisors, or Chiefs think this is acceptable within the dispatch center: the place where the calls for service are received and radio traffic is coordinated? In a crisis, everyone, field & public, turns to the Telecommunicators. Shouldn't the best Telecommunicators train the new hires? In order the prepare trainees, Public Safety Telecommunicators MUST have every skill, tool, and *certification* available.

It's just that simple.

For those who don't have the opportunity to become CTO certified first, it can be overwhelming. Sue Pivetta's book *The Exceptional Trainer* should be mandatory reading for all trainers. Trainers should take advantage of co-workers, dispatch website chat-rooms (for trainer boards), and read trade journals. Know your department policies & procedures; not just for the communications center, but for field personnel as well. Understanding how firefighters handle a missing unit call (mayday), how the local county emergency medical services responds to a mass casualty incident, or how the information needed by your department's SWAT team for a hostage incident is useful data to incorporate in your dispatcher training is crucial.

Trainers must be able to teach all skills that potentially could be required as part of the daily job. If your agency has access to DMV files, warrants, missing or wanted persons, boats, guns,

by Diana Sprain

restraining orders, or many of the other local, state, or national data bases, then you must train your Telecommunicator staff to the minimal levels required by state and federal law. Law enforcement agencies with access to the National Crime Information Center NCIC) data bases must be certified to use the system within six months of their initial hire date and bi-annually thereafter. As previously discussed, the Department's Terminal Agency Coordinator (TAC) is responsible for the overall training of personnel who have any duties relating to access to NCIC, State, regional, or local data systems. In-house data bases require training also. These files may include local arrest and/or contact history, hunting & fishing records, court records, prior case files, citations and field identifications, and miscellaneous information (timekeeping, maps, and historical data).

Trainers need to know the various pieces of equipment and software within dispatch. Text telephone devices (TTY/TDD), phones, radios, copiers/faxes, intercom systems, logging machines, audio playback devices, 9-1-1 screens, computer-aided dispatch, Internet search programs, aircraft monitoring programs, unit tracing devices, gps, etc. are used in the daily duties. Knowledge of operating and use of each is important.

Trainers should also become certified for emergency medical dispatching and Cardiopulmonary Resuscitation if they work in a center that provides pre-arrival medical instructions. Fire dispatchers should become familiar with the Incident Command System (ICS) and the National Incident Management System (NIMS). Those programs can be taught on-line or in person. Does your department use any type of incident card guidelines? Trainees should become familiar with the protocol cards system, if one is utilized in the agency.

Can a person interested in a dispatching career get training before becoming an employee of a department? Field personnel can attend colleges to get certification in firefighting, law enforcement, or as an EMT or paramedic. This brings to light our profession's lack of pre-employment training availability in an institution of higher learning. Community colleges and universities offer course work for law enforcement, fire science, and

What is Your Emergency? The History of Public Safety Dispatching in America

emergency medical services but public safety communications (dispatching) education is a rare bird, indeed. How many departments encourage high school students to pursue a career as a dispatcher? Why isn't a degree in emergency communications available at every college that offers a criminal justice or firefighting program? Have you ever seen a cop or firefighter walking around without a radio? For that matter, prehospital care programs (paramedic, EMT) should have emergency medical dispatching certification (along with a basic dispatch) for those same reasons.

In the article, *9-1-1, An Emerging 'Hidden' Career,* Sue Pivetta writes, "One common cry from 9-1-1 Trainers is, 'They didn't know what they were getting into.' The excitement of being a 9-1-1 Hero quickly fades thought the rigors of shift work, overtime, crisis situations, strenuous multitasking, and on the job training in a high stress environment where mistakes can be deadly. OJT is often referred to as 'learning to play the violin in public.' Had the candidates received entry level career training, the prospects of being, tested, hired, and thriving in the environment haven proven to be significant. Not only does the college or high school 9-1-1 graduate know 'what they were getting into' they jump start their training, improve the current bleak retention rates for new hires, and save the Comm Center funds and time."

I would add the training time for new hires might be reduced. The toll on current communications center working short-handed, or covering open shifts while trainers are off the floor in the classroom setting, is incredible. Informed trainees mean fewer dropouts in the training process. Let's face it, our profession has a dismal record when it comes to successful training of new dispatch personnel. We brag how only the top 3-5% of the population can handle the job, and when we sift through applications and finally have someone walk through the door on the first day, we make it difficult for that person to pass the training program and make their probation. Our trainees can be subjected to a training environment that can almost be called hostile. Instead of helping new Telecommunicators, co-workers can be standoffish with the mindset of 'I had to learn the hard way, why shouldn't he/she be able to do the same?' Every career day at a school (at any level) must include Public Safety Dispatching because no matter how far our technology advances, no matter how healthy our society may get, crime or fires or stupidity won't disappear. 911 will be necessary and that means dispatchers.

Until dispatching as a whole changes their stand on recruitment techniques and training, our communications centers will continue to work understaffed, stressed out, and short-tempered.

Having it all: the white picket fence, 2.5 kids, and a happy spouse

Once a dispatcher has made it past the probation date, he or she needs to learn how to balance their professional life with their private. Read any study involving public safety personnel and the statistics of divorce, alcoholism, drug use, and domestic violence rates are terrible. You're almost doomed from the start!

Putting family first is important. But how can one accomplish this, especially when shift work means working alternate hours, weekends and holidays? Some agencies require vacation sign-ups a year in advance while others only ask for a two-week notice for time off requests. Be honest with family or significant others. Explain the shift bid process and time-off requests in advance. If you decide to apply for a dispatcher job, your family needs to be made aware of what the entire application process is. If you accept the job, he or she needs to understand the commitment you will take for the training time and what will happen during your probation. There is the chance one can fail training and be out of a job.

Once you start, sit down and have a chat with your partner. Explain what the job is and what you will be doing as part of your training. Tell them about overtime, mandatory & voluntary. How does your agency handle sick leave or time off requests? There will be holidays when you have to work: including Christmas.

My son grew up with Christmas celebrated on the 22, the 23rd, the 24th, the 25th, and the 26th depending on our days off.

What is Your Emergency? The History of Public Safety Dispatching in America

He still had presents, a tree, lights, and time with family. We made a tradition of driving around the neighborhood to look at Christmas lights. The same went for Thanksgiving, 4th of July and birthdays. The important part was spending it with him. One or both of us (my husband was a paramedic / firefighter back then) seemed to be working. It is the nature of the job.

You'll miss school functions, church socials, kid's sports, birthday parties, and have to take vacations in off-times until you build up some seniority. Once you've completed your training & probation, you will be assigned a shift. Eventually, we all move up the seniority ladder as others leave and new folks are hired. This also allows us to have the opportunity to get better shifts. Remember, not everyone wants the day shift with weekends off. Unusual circumstances, such as disasters or major incidents may require cancellation of days off or vacation time.

"When you have nothing but your imagination, you create that evil scene in your mind": dispatcher stress and burnout

Public Safety Telecommunicators from day one work in an environment under a microscope. Every phone call is logged, every radio transmission is recorded, each incident is documented, and every event is scrutinized. When any incident goes sideways, the first step of the administration is to request a copy of the radio or phone tape. It is said that the job of a dispatcher is a roller-coaster of controlled chaos interrupted by insanity with the occasional break of calm. Every shift brings something different. That is the reason most Telecommunicators enjoy their jobs.

Human beings are meant to handle a certain amount of stress. How much is normal for one person compared to another varies according to many factors including socioeconomical, physical, physiological, and environmental. When life gets too much for any one person to cope with, we say that person is 'stressed out', but what does that really mean?

Webster's Dictionary defines stress as: "a condition typically characterized by symptoms of mental and physical tension or strain, as depression or hypertension that can result from a reaction to a situation in which a person feels threatened, pressured, etc." Stress symptoms can be minimal, causing a dispatcher to vent after disconnecting a telephone call, or range to the severe symptoms which may lead to 'burn-out' and eventual resignation from the job.

Individual incidents may impact a dispatcher and stick with her/him for the rest of their life. An example of such an event is a line-of-duty death or a call involving a child that ends in a fatality. One such incident occurred in March of 2009 when four Oakland (CA) police officers were killed, two during a traffic stop and two more during the entry to the building where the suspect was barricaded. Another example was the extreme loss of life during the rescue efforts in New York City on September 11th. What can the dispatch do but emphasize to a caller that the fire department *is* responding with lights and sirens, as the telecommunicator did in the case of an Oildale (CA) residential fire in which an eighteen month-old boy lost his life in June of 2013. In each case, the dispatchers did their jobs, obtaining necessary information to get the resources to the scene.

In Allen Kate's book, *CopShock,* the chapter on Police Dispatchers has an in-depth interview with dispatcher Jan Meyers. She explains how the job took its toll on her physical and mental health: "It's hard for a lot of people to accept that dispatchers can get PTSD. Because when you say a dispatcher has PTSD they get a critical look on their face like, 'What the hell, how does that happen? When you have nothing but your imagination, you create that evil scene in your mind, and when you see crime photos of it later, you look at them and say, 'Oh my God, it's not as nearly as bad as I pictured it."

Kate specifically identifies nine factors that affect dispatchers in the book *CopShock*. They are:

- Lack of control over their work schedule and duties
- Poor diet
- Night shifts that interrupt proper sleep patterns
- Lack of life outside the job
- Striving for perfection

- Lack of proper training
- False expectations and beliefs

Kate believes that these factors can lead to burn-out. How long does it take for a dispatcher to become stressed out enough to have a break-down or burn-out? That depends on the individual. In his book, Kates lists some of the more common signs & symptoms of burn-out:

- Feelings of anger and resentment towards supervisors
- Poor appetite or increase in eating
- Insomnia
- Stomachaches
- Headaches
- Constipation
- Feelings of worthlessness
- Cynicism
- Depression
- An inability to concentrate
- A sense of being overwhelmed
- Becoming forgetful
- Thoughts of suicide
- Recklessness and loss of control

Before a dispatcher gets to the point of burn-out, which isn't the same thing as Post Traumatic Stress Disorder (PTSD), he or she should talk to a trusted family member, friend, or take advantage of the agency's confidential counseling program. Take advantage and use your vacation time instead of letting it build up. Learn to keep work and the communications center. It's easy to want to discuss those strange or exciting calls with your family or friends but try to keep work and home separate. It's fine to join associates, go to meetings, get involved with internal activities but you still need to enjoy hobbies, go to a movie or continue to perform the activities you did before you became a dispatcher.

by Diana Sprain

"Please when will the medics get here? I can't breathe." The women pleaded. She was gasping for air and getting worse by the second from the time I had answered her frantic 911 call in the middle of the night. Her address displayed on the automated location identification (ALI) and I'd confirmed it with her. Too bad she lived in a secured apartment building on the third floor. The fire fighters and firefighter/paramedics had to force the door open to get inside her unit. I stayed on the line with her, actually hearing the guys bang on the door through the open telephone line. I heard one more gasp and the phone dropped. The crew was informed over the radio that the patient had probably lost consciousness. I heard the firemen break the door and announce themselves. A short time later the ambulance was transporting code three (lights & sirens) to the hospital but it was too late. She had died of an acute asthmatic attack.

I felt awful.

Another call that stuck with me was a baby not breathing. A co-worker answered a 911 call for a baby-not-breathing. The mother was hysterical, begging the dispatcher to tell her what to do. My co-worker tried to give medical instructions but our agency didn't provide the service and she wasn't trained to perform this duty. Frustrated she handed the call over to me. At that time, I was still a certified Emergency Medical Technician (and moon-lighting as an EMT on my days off). The mother was crying hysterically and in the background I could hear the father punching walls and screaming. Police patrol units, a fire engine, and the department's firefighter/paramedics were all enroute code three. I knew in my heart from the family telling me how they found the child cold, blue, and lifeless in his crib that the baby was gone, still one can't tell the parents that over the phone. I did what I could, even as the mother yelled at me to help her.

Those calls happened in the late eighties and I've never forgotten those voices. If only those women had called sooner, maybe the asthmatic and the infant would have made it. I went on after I hung up to handle more calls and dispatch other events. No rest or break; same for other bad nights. That was just the way it was for a long time. It's not as if the agencies didn't allow us to get

What is Your Emergency? The History of Public Safety Dispatching in America

out of dispatch after a rough event, but sometimes the *staffing or activity level* prohibited one from doing so right away. That was the reality. The same types of incidents occurs every day throughout the US. How does one get away to decompress when the center is only staffed with one dispatcher? Ask a supervisor or whoever is tasked to provide breaks, to cover for a short while.

If one works in a medium to large agency, then it is possible to leave the dispatch floor after a stressful telephone call or radio incident. This is not always the case in a small department. Many departments offer Employee Aid Plans, or some type of confidential counseling, available at any time. For a major incident, most departments now have debriefing sessions. A debriefing takes place within a few days of the incident, off-site, and is mentored by trained Critical Incident Stress Debriefing (CISD) personnel. During the meeting any involved personnel are invited to attend and talk about the event, discuss how the call was handled, the aftermath, feelings, and any difficulties he/she is having dealing with it. Anything said stays in that room and is strictly confidential. CISD members can also respond at the time of the incident in the event of line-of-duty deaths. Many agencies now require dispatch personnel to attend such briefings in the event of a line-of-duty death or major incident.

In 1984 one fire department's policy & procedure was in-depth in reference to a line-of-duty (LOD) death. CISD team members were contacted by the dispatchers and sent to the affected firehouses. A book was made, with check-lists on everything to do all the way up to and including the funeral procession arrangements. Too bad no one thought to include the communications personnel at any point.

Thankfully, that attitude is changing. Dispatchers are slowly being recognized as part of the team. Why? I believe it is more due to the technical aspects of the job. No longer can a field responder be called in to relieve Telecommunicators at a telephone or radio console as in 'the old days' when all activities were recorded on paper. The computerized, digitalized radio & dispatch systems require in-depth training, time most field personnel aren't willing to deal with just to cover for a short time in the 'radio room' any longer. Also consider many communications center have become regional dispatch centers requiring knowledge of multiple jurisdictions.

The multijurisdictional/regional dispatch center creates unique problems. Dispatch personnel may not get to know the field personnel as their counterparts in single agency communications centers do. Not having personal knowledge of field unit habits and/or voice recognition can lead to potential problems. For example, a blind transmission is defined when a unit transmits without identifying herself to the dispatcher. In an agency where dispatchers have the opportunity to interact face-to-face with field personnel, Telecommunicators develop the ability to match that voice with an individual. Although this is not always possible in large single agencies, working a regular shift with the same officers/firefighters may allow the same skill set.

We know that the dispatchers take a line-of-duty death just as hard as any co-worker of the law enforcement officer, firefighter, EMT, or paramedic. In some cases, even more. The second-guessing goes deep. *Could I have handled the call differently? Sent more cover, answered that call for help sooner, or figured out which person had sent the blind transmission a little quicker?*

The "Monday-Morning Quarterbacks" (also known as the press) replaying the 911 calls or radio tapes over & over on the news don't help. What can one do if this option is not immediately available? How can the news playing tapes impact a telecommunicator? Consider the example from the 1991 Oakland-Berkeley Firestorm (also known as the Tunnel Fire). One call-taker spoke with a woman across the San Francisco Bay. The female caller wanted to know if she should evacuate. It was doubtful the fire would jump the massive Bay to reach her residence and the call-taker told her not to worry. The media manipulated phone recording to air the call-taker telling the woman not to evacuate. The fact that she was well out of the danger zone was lost in the translation, causing an outcry from the public who never heard the entire transcript.

Talk with a trusted co-worker or family member about your feelings. Seek out a church figure. If a CISD session is offered at a later date take advantage of the opportunity and attend it. One must remember any confidential information must remain so.

Burn-out also occurs from working conditions. Under-staffed, overworked, low pay, and/or, no acknowledgment as a valid member of the Public Safety team are the most common complaints from dispatch personnel. The fall-out from the housing market crash resulted in many agencies having to tighten their budgets. As personnel retired or resigned, open positions were not filled putting an extra burden on the remaining staff in the Communications Center. Add to this, the increasing expectations of the public in general and it is easy to see how America's Public Safety Telecommunications have gone from a pool of veteran personnel to a profession where many aren't expected to last beyond their sixth year much less retirement.

On the Fire Side: Incident Dispatch Teams

An Incident Dispatch Team (IDT) consists of dispatch personnel who respond to the incident command posts during wildland fires or major incidents. No longer do Public Safety supervisors need to pull field personnel to handle the radios at an incident command post. Specially trained dispatchers respond along with fire command personnel, to the incident command post. The dispatchers manage the radio traffic, documenting as they go along on laptops (or paper) pre-loaded with the agency's computer-aided dispatch system complete with the incident command system (ICS) forms.

In addition to the CAD logging, dispatch track units on large maps, update status boards, and fill-in command staff of critical needs coming in on the radio. To become a member of an Incident Management Team, one needs to have at least a year of fire dispatching experience and have a good working knowledge of the Incident Command System (ICS) and the National Incident Command System (NIMS). In addition, completion of the National Emergency Management Authority (FEMA) courses in ICS and NIMS are recommended. The exact classes may vary according to the individual agencies. One department that utilizes dispatchers in

by Diana Sprain

the field for major fire and emergency medical incidents is the Metropolitan Area Communications Center in Centennial, Colorado. MetComm first opened in 2006 and handling 15,000 calls in 2011 & 42,000 phone calls. The agency is a secondary PSAP, taking care of the fire and medical services. MetComm dispatchers are certified as Emergency Medical Dispatchers, Emergency Fire Dispatchers, in ICS, and NIMS. In an official METCOMM April 28th overview, the team is described as:

"MetCom's IDT members are qualified through an in-house training academy which covers a wide range of material from the basics of firefighting to building a communications plan. All members are required to be certified through ICS 400. The team also has 1 FEMA Type 3 COML, 2 COML trainees, 1 NWCG COML Trainee, 3 NWCG COMT Trainees and 1 Type 3 Logistics Section Chief. All members of the IDT are also on Arapahoe County's Type 4 IMT."

"When deployed, all IDT members are equipped with a full set of Nomex bunker and wildland gear, allowing them to safely function on scene. As a single resource, the members will bring a kit that includes a laptop computer, printer, camera, GPS, VHF radio programming equipment, internet access, weather software including radar & lightning data, a cache of ICS forms and a small office supply kit."

"In support of our agencies, the IDT operates two fully-equipped response vehicles and two SUVs. The primary response vehicle is designated as "IDT1" which is an ambulance-sized communications unit. It has all of the capabilities of a single resource dispatcher with added computer capability, whiteboard walls for resource tracking, onboard generator, cell phones, fax machine, two 800 MHz and two VHF mobile radios and most importantly, an ICRI Tactical Gateway. The ICRI allows the team members to bridge dissimilar radio systems or frequency bands together on scene to facilitate interoperability."

A January 1999 U.S. Fire Administration Technical Report on firefighter communications examined the man aspects of the topic. The author recommended all field personnel carry portable radios designed to be used in field conditions. The report specified better

What is Your Emergency? The History of Public Safety Dispatching in America

training for firefighters in the use of radio communications with standardized message formats. Even more important to communications, the author advised:

"Dispatchers area a critical component of the communications loop. They must have an in-depth understanding of the fireground environment to ensure their ability to triage messages according to their importance and re-broadcast any vital messages to all of those enroute to, or at the scene…Dispatchers should be continually involved in fireground communication by actively listening for transmissions that might go unnoticed, reporting changes to the normal response order, and conveying messages among responding units. Care should be taken, however, to minimize fireground radio traffic from being overridden by powerful transmitters at dispatcher centers."

The report suggested sending a 'Field Communications Unit' to multiple alarms incidents. This person would manage the radio with dispatchers in the field. In essence, the author was referring to Incident Dispatch Teams. The one disadvantage to having outside dispatch personnel running another agency's incident is lack of familiarity with the computer systems. This is illustrated by a report in the 2007 southern California firestorms. The team who studied the 23 simultaneous fires noted:

Problems emerged at one center as expanded dispatch teams were brought in from out of area. One respondent explained that in California there are multiple databases and multiple agreements in place and available to the dispatch system. The system is inherently redundant and the duplication often creates confusion and a potential for recordkeeping mishaps. For dispatch staff to succeed, they must be knowledgeable about all of the databases and the agreements. When expanded dispatchers come from out of area or out of region, they struggle with the steep learning curve this complex system of databases and agreements poses."

Training can be provided via the individual agencies. A great resource is via the web at www.incidentdispatch.net

Emergency Medical Dispatcher

Provide pre-arrival emergency medical instructions to callers. The instructions start from the moment the Emergency Medical Dispatcher (EMD) answers the telephone call until the First Responder arrives on scene. Emergency Medical Dispatchers must take a certified course on EMD.

The International Association of Emergency Dispatch (IAED) is the oldest US association to oversee training, certification, and re-certification of emergency medical dispatchers. The IAED requires Cardiopulmonary Resuscitation (CPR) certification and recertification every two years.

EMD's use their knowledge to talk callers through starting CPR, delivering babies, controlling bleeding, or any other medical problem that can arise. Departments may require Telecommunicators be become certified Emergency Medical Technicians (EMTs) in order to advance to handling other radio traffic, such as life flight helicopters.

Emergency Medical Dispatcher training can be done via individual departments, regional emergency medical authorities, some community colleges, the Associated Public Safety Communications Officials (APCO), the International Association of Emergency Dispatchers (IAED), and many different private training companies.

Tactical Dispatcher

"Dispatch, 5L42, 10-21 residence and have the RP step outside."

"5L42, 10-4." A few moments later...

"5L42, dispatch."

"Dispatch, 5L42, go ahead."

"5L42, the subject refuses to step out and won't allow any family to leave either. He also says he is armed with a handgun. I'm still on landline getting additional."

What is Your Emergency? The History of Public Safety Dispatching in America

There came a time in my career when I looked for something more, another challenge. I was fortunate in that the department I was working for at that time in my career included dispatchers as part of the SWAT team. I applied and became a member of the team. All new recruits were required to go through a 12 week course which included SWAT survival, shooting, intelligence gathering, hazardous materials, and hostage negotiations. We had to meet a basic physical fitness requirement. Later, I was sent to a Tactical Dispatcher class at San Jose PD. We manned the command post and worked the incident at dispatch. Other dispatchers I've spoken with have even worked with the negotiators.

Dispatchers negotiate everyday as part of their job to obtain data regarding call location, details about the type of incident (fire, emergency medical services, or law), persons involved, etc. We teach dispatch trainees the important facts to gather and in which order. It was only natural that Telecommunicators become part of the SWAT (Special Weapons and Tactics) Teams.

Having a natural ear for voice tones and speaking with people, the first dispatcher probably became the unofficial 'third' members of the Negotiator team. He, or she, gathered intelligence on the suspect and scene and provided that information to the Secondary Negotiator. In time, a few trend-setters brought dispatchers officially on the team to run the radio traffic. Along with the communications center personnel, Tactical Medics (TEMS) joined the crew. In some agencies, *all* team members go through the same SWAT course, the reasoning being the team works better when everyone knows each other's job.

Tactical Dispatch training can be obtained through State POST, the Associated Public Safety Communications Officials (APCO), or via many private law enforcement training companies.

Supervisors

Dispatcher Supervisors can be on different levels and are defined by the individual department. One common type is a Lead Dispatcher. A Lead can be a dispatcher with a certain amount of time on the job or a person who has indicated he or she would be willing to take an active role in dealing with problems should a supervisor not be available. An Acting Supervisor is similar to a Lead. I've been an Acting Supervisor when our Supervisor has been on leave.

Some agencies have dedicated shift Supervisors. These people make certain the shifts are covered, handle immediate problems, and oversee their assigned shift. They act as liaisons to the field personnel. Depending on the agencies, they may have special duties. They may perform annual evaluations for the personnel on their shift. They may spend some time working a dispatch position.

Managers oversee the department. They usually have hiring and firing authority – or at least can recommend this to the Chief. They may perform the annual evaluations, get the budget together, give presentations to other departments, and perform other duties as assigned.

When I made the decision to apply for a Supervisor, I knew it would be major change in my life. At the time, the Supervisors were expected to fill-in if the shift was short-handed. My special project was training. I also helped cover for the TAC (see below) when she was on leave. I wrote the performance evaluations for the trainees and for the staff on my assigned shift. I had to attend staff meetings and shift briefings. I actually brought work home. It was very stressful.

When things went wrong, eyes turned to me for guidance. The ball that rolled downhill stopped at my feet. I had to learn to be diplomatic. At first, I was Gung-Ho to make changes. My shift complained about my attitude. After a discussing with the boss, I mellowed out. Changing the world, or a shift, happens in baby steps. Supervising former peers, and friends, is a delicate act.

One way to get supervisor experience is to be a Lead or Acting supervisor. This position only handles immediate issues.

Terminal Agency Coordinator (TAC)

The Terminal Agency Coordinator is the liaison between a department and the State Terminal Agency. Any department which

What is Your Emergency? The History of Public Safety Dispatching in America

wishes access to data bases for investigative reasons; to send and/or receive administrative messages or teletypes; or to enter, update, locate, or cancel items in any data base maintained by the Department of Justice, including criminal history, vehicles, property, missing persons, guns, etc, must agree to the rules set by the FBI. One of these rules is having a liaison, or Terminal Agency Coordinator, designated for that department.

TAC's are responsible for overseeing all training of personnel who see, hear, or have access to any records. The Terminal Agency Coordinator must validate records and work with the IT department's Local Agency Security Officer (LASO) to make certain no unauthorized persons gain access to records or use them in any illegal manner. TAC can have assistants (ATACs) to help in the performance of their duties.

TAC's must ensure that information entered in any of the data bases is correct and current. Every two-to-three years, operational and technical audits are performed by the State Control Agency, as mandated by the Federal Bureau of Investigation. Problems or possible concerns are identified and most be corrected by the TAC.

As an example of TAC or ATAC duties, I have been responsible for handling the annual State audits. I make certain all personnel who access the State or federal data bases receive initial and annual training. I have to document the training received. I need to make certain the paperwork documenting the backgrounds for our dispatchers and officers have been properly completed. I update dispatch policies and procedures as they relate to NCIC/NCJIS. I ensure that all of our field personnel are trained tot he proper use of the various NCIC/NCJIS systems by providing live and internet-based training. When I have time, I attend State meetings of the Technical Committee to keep up with and give my inout of changes to the State system. All of this is in addition to my day-to-day duties as a working dispatcher.

by Diana Sprain

Chapter Thirteen

The Survey

To get a rough picture of our profession, I came up with a non-scientific survey consisting of twenty-four questions. The topics below include why we (Public Safety Telecommunicators) become dispatchers, the hiring process, training, and information about the departments we work at. I asked for anonymity in the responses hoping to get honest answers. Along with the returned surveys, I received some comments – of which, I've included selected anecdotes in the book.

I didn't ask the usual breakdown questions that you see in usual surveys regarding race, annual income, or age. I decided it wasn't worth it because not everyone would answer those queries. I normally skip the race/financial data questions - or if they are mandatory, put phony stuff just to skew the data. So, why bother?

Here are the questions I asked, in the order I asked them. The numbers don't add to 100% because some respondents gave answers for more than one agency. Percentages have been rounded up or down to the nearest even number

Why did you become dispatcher?

> Gateway to other Public Safety positions **10%**
> Job allowed me to pursue education (once probation over) **5%**
> Fell in to the job (i.e. asked to learn position to cover for vacations, etc.) **29%**
> Liked the pay and benefits **10%**
> Heard about the profession and it sounded interesting **37%**

The tallied on this question were surprising, with respondents 'heard about the job' outnumbered the 'fell into the job' category. In retrospect, this is good. Our profession as a whole is recruiting and students are considering public safety communications a career. In fact, agencies are making television and Internet commercials advertising dispatching. Las Vegas Metropolitan Police Department (NV) ran an ad on a local cable television channel when it was ready to accept telecommunicator applications. YouTube has a dozen such recruitment 'ads' for dispatchers.

Did you work in the Public Safety field prior to becoming a Dispatcher

No **54%**
Yes, as a firefighter **11%**
Yes, as a law enforcement officer **10%**
Yes, as an EMT or Paramedic (private or 9-1-1 contracted) **12%**
Yes, in the military (position other than those listed here) **82%**
Yes, as an Air Traffic Controller **0%**
Yes, dispatching in the private sector (tow truck, taxi, trucking, etc.) **82%**

Over half of the dispatchers who responded began their careers in Public Safety as entry level. 33% had prior experience as a first responder before taking over the radio in dispatch. An impressive 82% of the surveys returned checked off the private sector experience. Does being a tow-truck or taxi dispatcher help? I believe any radio experience is helpful and I'd take a person with a radio background over a help-desk background.

As part of your hiring process, did you (check all that apply)

Take a written test **61%**
Participate in an oral board **69%**
Take a drug test **44%**
Take a polygraph **20%**

Take a psychological test **51%**
Take a hearing test **49%**
Take a medical exam **56%**
Have fingerprint background done **56%**
Have a investigative background **68%**
Have a second interview done **54%**
Do a practical exam (via a simulator) **54%**

It's a funny thing how the hiring process for dispatchers has changed over the decades. It used to be less was more. A person's word was good enough to get a job offer, but not any more: our lawsuit happy society is too quick to file paperwork than to take responsibility for our own actions. Some professions have changed how they do business as a result (medicine running extra tests 'just in case'). Only 20% of the agencies required a polygraph exam yet 69% faced an oral board. I was surprised to find none of the categories had 100% response.

If you NO LONGER work as a dispatcher, why did you leave? ** I amended this to later read 'If you left the profession and later returned, what was your reason for initially leaving?'

Finished education and moved on to new career **3%**
Became first responder (law enforcement officer/firefighter/paramedic/EMT) **0%**
Enrolled in military **0%**
Spouse relocated for his/her job **0%**
Repetitive injury/other work-related injury **0%**
Didn't pass probation / termination **0%**
Burned out **0%**
Position eliminated **7%**

I only wish I could have put the survey out to all first responders. I think I'd have received a greater number of varied answers. Unfortunately, no one expanded on the 'position eliminated' choice. I personally worked with a couple of dispatchers who qualified for choices 'b' and 'e'.

What is Your Emergency? The History of Public Safety Dispatching in America

Working in the communications center has become a stepping stone to field work. You learn the area, the personnel, and the policies & procedures. As for the work-related injuries, it is a sad-fact of life for our profession that technology comes with a price. Keyboarding and mousing lead to repetitive injuries – especially in departments that don't provide ergonomic workstations.

In reference to ride-alongs at your agency…

Are ride-alongs for trainees only? **37%**
Are fire ride-alongs only with fire engines? **0%**
Are fire ride-alongs only with medics on ambulances? **5%**
Are ride-alongs allowed any time with supervisor approval? **56%**
Are you kidding? Ride-alongs are for patients and prisoners only. **5%**

One can see that trainees area allowed to get out and 'see the world' and some agencies do give dispatch personnel the chance to escape for a few hours on occasion. Departments that encourage communications center employees to spend some time in the field, however little that may be, help dispatchers – and field units – to have a better working relationship. Being told what the 'other side does' verses *seeing* the actual duties makes a tremendous difference in both call-taking and dispatching. Why does an officer take so long to answer a status check? What does a fire company do when they perform an initial size-up? Why does a medical call take longer than a trauma call? Getting out and seeing problem areas, common landmarks, schools, parks, marinas, or campgrounds will help in future events.

Scheduling rides with all three services a quarter is ultimately the best for a combined PSAP. For a fire/ems, one session with each service a month works. Sadly, some dispatchers reported flat refusals when asked if they could go out for a few hours at best.

by Diana Sprain

In reference to sit-alongs in dispatch...

The Public is allowed with prior Supervisor approval. **64%**
Law Enforcement Rookies are required to spend time in dispatch as scheduled by their FTOs. **49%**
Fire / EMS personnel are required to spend time in dispatch as scheduled by their FTOs. **24%**
Our field personnel are *shown* where dispatch is, so they can drop off paperwork and make requests. **24%**
We're lucky they know our phone number, let's not ask for miracles here. **17%**

    Public Safety Telecommunicators are probably the most transparent profession in all of public safety. Phone calls and radio traffic are recorded, call events are either on paper or documented by computer-aided dispatch systems, and even some dispatch centers are video-taped. There's not very much that a dispatcher does that isn't tracked, noted, signed, or doubled-checked. In many centers, their specific duties are even scheduled for each shift. That's a far difference from many field personnel. Members of the public and the media are often invited to take a seat and observe dispatchers at work. Many Citizens Academies now include a 'sit-along' session with a dispatcher.
    A minimal amount of hours in the communications center should be required of every public safety branch. Let's face reality here, until the field workers truly open their arms and welcome dispatchers into the circle of first responders, a free exchange of information and training won't occur. Telecommunicators *should* instruct the radio etiquette portion of field unit academies. t allows the ability to explain why radio traffic is formatted or what requirements are for various inquiries. Time after time, during the actual major incident, the person relied upon to be calm and to know what to do is the dispatcher.
    Having had more than my fair share of first responders sit alongside me to observe, it's amazing how many leave with a new understanding of the Telecommunicator's job. Two recent wardens watch me juggle the phones, a flight, 25 channels, CAD, inquiry

What is Your Emergency? The History of Public Safety Dispatching in America

requests, and still explain to them what I was doing. After eight hours, I told the two recruits they could always apply for dispatch if they decided the field wasn't for them. The usual response is a firm 'No way – I couldn't handle what you do'.

There will always be the odd person who doesn't want to be inside, resents the time with the dispatcher, and is closed minded about the experience. You just can't change that person's opinion but the majority will walk away with a little more respect about the job.

Training is important. When it comes to training, how does your Department handle training?

We have a formal academy program, consisting of _____ hours total, graduating a dispatcher who is ready to answer a call with minimal guidance.

We have a mixture of classroom and one-on-one live mentoring broken up in to phases consisting of roughly _____ hours.

We have an informal training process, with a new hire assigned a trainer. They work closely together, until the trainer clears the new hire to work alone. This takes roughly _____ hours.

Our training is on-the-job. We all help the new person learn, answering questions as new situations come up.

I had to break this response down. Here are the percentages of the responses (25% didn't answer this question).
1-14 hours: **40%**
40-60 hours: **none**
61-80 hours: **5%**
81-100 hours: **none**
101- to 120 hours: **none**
121 to 180 hours: **2%**
181 to 240 hours: **7%**
241 to 500 hours: **22%**
501 to 1000 hours: **15%**
1001 to 1050 hours: **5%**

1051 hours to 2000 hours: **7%**
2001 to 2500 hours: **2%**
No response: **25%**

All I can say is wow. For what we as a group do, we need to SCREAM at the travesty of our unpreparedness for our job. Cosmetologists and Massage Therapists are required to have more training yet Public Safety Dispatchers must make snap decisions and the wrong one can have deadly consequences.

During your training time, did you (circle all that apply):

Take any quizzes or tests **63%**
View any films **2%**
Listen to training tapes 59%
Given any hand-outs (radio codes, criminal codes, CAD Codes, etc.) **76%**
Provided with a copy of the agencies general policies and procedures **80%**
Provided with a copy of the Communications Center policies and procedures **73%**
Taken on tour of your building **61%**
Taken on tour of response area **66%**
Taken to local (neighboring) PSAPS **34%**
Shown department precincts or fire houses **63%**
Introduced to department Administration personnel **83%**
Given training outline **66%**
Given regular feedback on your progress **71%**
Allowed to respond to negative evaluations **66%**
Give Daily Observation Reports (DORs) with a place to note your comments and a time to review them with your trainer **54%**

These answers had a few surprises. One would think that every agency took new hires on a tour, but nope. How do their new folks find their way around - by Braille or colored tape on the floor? It is a shame that in this day some trainees are not provided with feedback during the 'training' period. How can any Dispatch Supervisor let a new hire go when the dispatch trainee has not been given any written evaluations to track progress (or lack thereof)? Only 73-80% were given copies of policies & procedures. Let's hope the others at least knew where to read them, and if not maybe they worked for those departments where they *didn't* get introduced to the Administrative personnel. It's easier to keep under the proverbial radar if the head honchos don't know who you are.

As part of your duties as a dispatcher (select all that apply), you:

Work a call-taking position **90%**
Work a fire dispatching channel **7%**
Work an EMS channel **73%**
Work a law enforcement channel (9-1-1 PSAP) **90%**
Work full access to process NCIC, State, local inquiry, update, locates & clears **22%**
Work EMD (pre-arrival instructions) **15%**
Work inquiry-only NCIC channel **51%**
Work other law enforcement (non 9-1-1 PSAP) **46%**
Are a Civilian Training Officer (CTO) **61%**
Are a Tactical Dispatcher (SWAT team dispatcher) **63%**
Are a TERT Dispatcher (disaster response dispatcher) **29%**
Are a IDT Dispatcher (Wildland fire response certified) 34%
Do you make radio tapes **12%**
Do you teach in a formal dispatch academy **5%**
Do you teach in your agency's FTO (field personnel) Academy **15%**
Do you go and give presentations to citizens regarding your Communication Center **17%**
Do you participate in any special projects in-house **7%**
Do you participate in any special projects outside of your agency **2%**
Are you a member of APCO **12%**
Are you a member of NENA **12%**

by Diana Sprain

Have you ever served on a committee for APCO? **2%**
Have you served on a committee for NENA? **39%**
Have you been a officer for APCO? **17%**
Have you been an officer for NENA? **0%**
Have you ever attended an APCO convention? **5%**
Have you ever attended a NENA convention? **2%**

The duties of a Public Safety Telecommunicator consist of a varied list of duties and can be different from one agency to the next. In addition to the basic job of answering phone calls and co-coordinating radio traffic, dispatchers may handle records. Smaller agencies may require the Telecommunicators to answer request at a public counter. Dispatch may handle subpoena requests for radio recordings or documentation copies.

Training or co-coordinating the training of new hires can be tasked to line-dispatchers, supervisors, or a designated person. Tracking the progress of trainees can be intensive, especially if doing this while working a regular shift. Agencies that have access to the FBI data bases mandate detailed training of operators and bi-annual recertification as well. Getting involved with APCO or NENA is a wonderful way to keep current with trends and new ideas.

On occasion, Telecommunicators may be assigned to teach within the in-house academy. Some departments request dispatchers for citizen meetings, to explain procedures or discuss a neighborhood concern as it relates to communications. There may be special projects, such as working on a policy & procedure or assisting with an agency certification.

Many dispatchers are involved in the profession outside of the department. National organizations often rely on volunteers to staff offices, serve on committees, or participate by helping at conferences or events. National membership usually comes with journals and message board access. Networking is a great way to connect with dispatchers in other areas. Most of us have to pay our own dues or conference fees. Still, the number of working dispatchers who are members of APCO or NENA is low. More of us need to join the organizations and get involved if we want real changes in our profession.

Does your supervisor require you to (circle all that apply)

Attend a briefing prior to sitting down at your position **7%**
Check your email at least once a day **58%**
Voice concerns via email or in writing **36%**
Respond to complaints via email or writing **34%**
Pass on important information on a regular basis **10%**
Have regular meetings with the dispatch staff to keep in touch with concerns or pass on management information **34%**
Have a clue about the daily activities of the job **29%**
Provide annual evaluations **16%**
Schedule training once probation is completed **22%**

    Some of these questions might seem outrageous, but to many of us the issues raised are not. Passing on information should be a regular part of the day, after all we work in *communications* but we all know better. How many times have we been taken off guard by the 'out of the blue' phone call by a member of the public inquiring on that new software they read about in the local newspaper that our department has, which can instantly point out a location in a community building to dispatch (huh??? When did we get *that???)*. How embarrassing to read about new hires in a police or fire blotter first, or even worse, the termination of an employee.
    I wrote response *'g' have a clue about the daily activities of the job* partly as a joke, not really thinking anyone would select this answer. Silly me…I know how many co-workers over the 25+ years I have been in the same room with who, once they passed probation somehow 'forgot' everything he or she was taught. How difficult can it be to recall main streets when there is a huge map of the City hanging up in dispatch? No radio dispatcher should have to break in and take over a 9-1-1 call to get suspect descriptions because the call-taker isn't doing his or her job, but it happens. Who forgets to change logging tapes, send ambulances, or ask if

anyone was in the burning building? Who misses an officer needs help call or forgets to check teletypes?

More departments send general notices via email, even doing the old fashioned 'read & sign' with a return receipt and an email is opened and read. Only pre-shift briefings in which current news is given out (over multiple shifts and days) ensures all dispatch personnel actually hear and understand important policy changes, key incidents, or new procedures. These should be followed with a real read and sign. This takes away the 'I didn't know or get that email' excuse.

How many of us do annual mandatory training for our agency on-line? The Human Resource Department may send an email with a list of on-line security classes and the deadline date for completing them, or just a reminder with a deadline date. It is then up to the individual to sort through a list of courses and complete each class on duty, between official functions. If you are lucky, you may get time off the floor to knock out the courses, or do them on your own time for credit.

Explain to me how only 16% of the respondents are provided with annual evaluations? If there is a problem, the agency has no leg to stand on when it comes to disciplinary procedures. An employee can claim they had no idea they were incompetent because no one ever gave them documented feedback. How is progressive discipline handled without any basic evaluations as a base?

As a Supervisor (Circle all that apply)

Work as a line dispatcher before you were promoted **56%**
Perform employee evaluations **58%**
Cover a radio channel when shift is short-handed **56%**
Work a call-taker position when shift is short-handed **54%**
Attend Administration meetings **54%**
Write Communications-related Policy & Procedures **56%**
Do dispatch scheduling **56%**
Approve time-off requests **49%**
Be the Terminal Agency Coordinator (TAC) **24%**

Be an Assistant TAC (ATAC) **22%**
Coordinate dispatcher training or run the dispatch training Academy **39%**
Teach the communications portion of the law enforcement, EMS, or firefighter portion of the Department's FTO program **41%**
Investigate complaints **51%**
Recommend discipline **51%**
Recommend termination **46%**
Discipline employees **10%**
Terminate employees **44%**
Attend conventions on the agencies expense account **51%**
Write policies and procedures **49%**
Manage the CAD system **29%**

    I looked back and should have broken this section up between line Supervisors and Managers. As a former Supervisor at a combined police & fire public safety answering point (PSAP), I know how much work can get piled up. The smaller the department, the more work the supervisor is assigned and in many cases he/she must delegate many of the duties to the dispatchers out of necessity. In larger departments, there can be multiple supervisors and acting supervisors to help out.
    Most folks said Dispatch Managers had authority to fire, with approval of the Chief, but the majority of communications center supervisors worked with or under a sworn person. Thankfully this mentality of requiring sworn personnel, fire or law enforcement, to manage the communications Center is changing. I believe the catalyst has been the emerging technologies in the decent decades of CAD, digital radio, and computerized telephones & consoles. No longer can a law enforcement officer or firefighter rotate an assignment through Dispatch and put on a headset to handle radio. Even writing communications center policies requires knowledge of the equipment and software which is more than many field personnel are willing to learn for a short term assignment.
    Many Supervisors are still expected to work the floor, covering for minimal staffing. In some cases, their schedules are

set to have partial days off the floor for administrative duties and the other days working at a console. Over half of the respondents said they investigated complaints and recommended disciplinary action. Most of the supervisors were assigned 'special projects' for the Department. These projects included being in charge of the dispatch training as a Training Coordinator; named Terminal Agency Coordinator or Assistant (TAC or ATAC), handling the communications center scheduling; being a liaison with local, regional, state or national organizations (including APCO and NENA); and, named the CAD system Administrator. These 'extra' duties weren't compensated.

If you are still employed as a dispatcher, what do you like best about your job?

Variable hours **10%**
Pay and benefits **19%**
Chance to save a life (EMD) **27%**
Never the same calls from day-to-day **51%**
Being part of the team **29%**

Over half of the respondents marked the best part of the job was the variety form shift to shift. Time or day is irrelevant. Fights, accidents, heart attacks, or fires don't care what time the clock displays or day of the week. Next was the feeling of being part of the team. A close choice was the opportunity to use emergency medical dispatching skills to save a life, in third place. Pay & benefits took fourth from the final selection, variable hours.

If you are still employed as a dispatcher, what do you dislike the most about your job?

24/7 job makes me miss out on a lot of family events **32%**
Having to put up with verbal abuse from citizen callers **24%**
Working chronically understaffed in dispatch **34%**
The lack of respect and acknowledgment from other Public Safety personnel **41%**

Not being considered a true First Responder **29%**

The winner here was *'d' the lack of respect and acknowledgment form other Public Safety personnel* at 41%. Again, we as a profession must take part of the blame. Firefighters, law enforcement officers, and emergency medical personnel each must be certified and maintain a minimal amount of continuing education. Dispatchers trained in emergency medical dispatching do need to maintain the certification requirements. There are states which have mandatory training for Telecommunicators, but this is NOT nationwide. Once our profession stands up for this change, I believe the attitude will be better and we'll be accepted as a true member of the first responder crowd.

That brings us to the second highest number of responses: working in an under-staffed dispatch center. This naturally leads to overtime – both voluntary and mandatory – which then brings us to the third choice, missing out in family events. Even though not being considered a first responder came in at number four, that choice really goes hand-in-hand with the first choice. Finally, the abuse by callers is part of the job, but it does take a toll on the call-taking staff. Over the years, recent studies have proven that cumulative stress does matter to Public Safety Dispatchers.

When it comes to training, are you (check all that apply):

Required to have any dispatcher training by your State? **49%**
Required to have any dispatcher training by your County? **12%**
Required to have any *certification* for law enforcement dispatching by your State's POST or via State regulations? **41%**
If the answer to question 4 is yes, how many hours? **See below.**

If you provide EMD (pre-arrival instructions), how many initial training hours do you   obtain and how many recertification hours   must you take? How often do you recert, and finally, are you required to do any continuing education credits EMD initial

Training is a sensitive subject. One can't have uncertified personnel providing medical 'advice' over the phones. Law enforcement and firefighters are required to receive annual training. What of dispatchers? Except for state requiring mandatory education, and the FBI's regulations as to operator certification, most of us are left behind when it comes to training after we are cleared to work on our own.

34% of the respondents receive 1 to 25 hours of initial training (this included fire, law, or ems). 12% received 26 to 50 hours; and, 2% sat in for 51 to 100 hours. Emergency Medical Dispatch training was specifically mentioned in the question but there were few responses. 24% reported receiving 1 to 24 hours of instruction while 12% said they received 25 to 50 hours.

Many of us agree that annual training is important to Public Safety Telecommunications staff. Technology, legislation changes, and department (and communications center) policies & procedures are dynamic. Every time a lawsuit is settled – in or out of court – our job changes. Technology is growing every year. Telecommunicators must keep up to date. How can dispatchers be knowledgeable without an avenue for information exchanges? Field personnel must show proof that they can shoot their firearms with a minimal amount of accuracy, understand which retardants to safely extinguish a chemical fire, and paramedics are required to re-certify every two years.

Of the dispatchers required to seek continuing education, 24% attended 1 to 24 hours, 7% earned 25 to 50 hours, and 2% were required to take 51 to 100 hours of training. None of the respondents specified if the training was strictly in-house or a combination of in-department and outside agency courses.

Do you get any pay raises?

Yes, annual cost of living raises **24%**
Yes, per Union contract. **29%**
Possible, the raises are merit based **24%**
Yes, but raises are frozen due to budget problems until further notice **22%**

What is Your Emergency? The History of Public Safety Dispatching in America

This is self explanatory – I only left out, 'No, we don't." as a choice. It's disturbing to see that duties continue to increase, inflation grows, and yet there are 22% of our dispatchers stuck without additional compensation. In some cases, pay was reduced or furloughs instituted.

Do you belong to a union?

Yes, I am part of a closed (mandatory) shop **34%**
No, I can join a union if I chose (open) shop **41%**
I live in a right to work State **10%**

For those who don't know what the term 'Right to Work' refers to, it means you don't have to join a union although any rules applied to union members must equally be applied to non-union members. Employers must follow Federal Labor Law standards. Always take a few minutes to read the posted Federal Labor Law posters, you might be surprised to learn what your, and your employers', right are.

We all need to think about retirement, how is your retirement handled by your agency?

They pay 100% of my retirement to a State retirement system **12%**
We split costs equally to a State retirement **56%**
I pay 100% of the costs to a State retirement **5%**
I pay a percentage to an IRA **2%**
Other **24%**

Always read the fine print. More agencies are switching to an employer/employee shared cost plan or a 401k-type retirement. Checkout your options and attend the meetings to understand your options. If one has a chance to join supplemental retirement programs such as deferred compensation, take advantage of this opportunity.

Health benefits are important. How does your agency dole out benefits for your family?

They cover 100% for me and my family **19%**
They cover me and my spouse, but I pay for my kids **10%**
They cover me, but I pay for my spouse and kids **24%**
I pay for all of us **29%**

How will the Affordable Care Act change the way government agencies provide health benefits to new employees and their dependants? Will the days of 100% coverage for all family members disappear? Medical premiums can be expensive. When you consider an agency that requires furloughs, freezes pay raises, and requires the employee to contribute to health plan premiums, that 'great' salary some how isn't as nice.

What is your job satisfaction? Select one

Can't be any better, I love my job **10%**
There's a few things I'd change but overall not bad. **58%**
It pays the bills, if I could get on something else I'd switch in a heartbeat. **10%**
I dread coming to work. **5%**
I hate my life and work sucks. **0%**

Most of the folks who answered the survey like their job. Some loved it and a few hated it. That is about right for the average communications center. There's always one person who wishes they worked somewhere else, but for various excuses won't leave (possibly suffering from burn-out) and on the other end of the curve the couple who think the position is fantastic. Those 'life is wonderful' people are either upbeat, the glass-is-half-full' types or still on probation.

What is Your Emergency? The History of Public Safety Dispatching in America

How many field personnel does your agency handle?

1-25 units **19%**
26-50 units **27%**
51-76 units **7%**
76 to 100 units 5%
101 to 150 units **5%**
151 to 200 units 10%
210 to 250 units **none**
251 to 500 **5%**
500+ units **2%**

Managing radio traffic is a major part of a Telecommunicator's position. How much radio traffic, the content, and procedures relating to the radio can speak miles for how busy a dispatcher is. Less than a dozen officers dealing with the day-to-day activities can be hectic when one also answers the phones. In contrast, larger agencies may restrict radio dispatchers from being on the phone due to the constant back & forth over the radio. What is the best ratio of dispatcher to field personnel? It strictly depends of average activity. On a busy holiday weekend, the department I work for can have 30-40 units all keeping busy on 23+ radio channels through-out the state. What I didn't ask, and I should have, was if the agency separated the call-taking and radio duties. I also should have asked for the ratio of dispatcher to field unit.

How many dispatchers does your agency have?

1 to 5 **5%**
6 to 10 **24%**
11 to 20 **15%**
21 to 30 **12%**
31 to 40 **7%**
41 to 50 **5%**
51 to 60 **0%**
61 to 70 **2%**
71 to 80 **0%**

81 to 90 **0%**
91 to 100 **0%**
101 to 125 **0%**
125+ **2%**

Staffing can make or break a communications center. Having 'warm bodies' in a center to show 'full staffing' on paper doesn't do any good. Should a trainee be allowed to work without trainer supervision is a powder keg waiting to blow up. What is the department's liability should a problem occur? The other cost in centers at minimal or below staffing levels is in the amount of sick leave used by personnel or overtime required to cover the spaces.

How many dispatch supervisors does your agency have?

1 to 5 **51%**
6 to 10 **10%**
11 to 20 **0%**
21 to 30 **5%**

It's nice to have a go-to person to troubleshoot problems on duty. When the supervisors aren't available, who takes care of issues? Many agencies allow for 'acting supervisors' to take over when a regular person is not on duty. In some cases, the acting supervisors are compensated but many departments don't pay for the extra duty.

What type of shifts does your dispatch center work?

5/8 **32%**
4/10 **22%**
3/12 plus 1 8 hour **10%**
24 hours (rotating Kelly) **none**
Other **24%**

The majority of us still work an eight-hour day, five days a week. The 'Other' was mix of so many varieties it made my head spin. Ten hour shifts, four days a week are also popular. Although no one answered a rotating 24 hour, I do know of one agency that at one tie did have its dispatchers on a fire department (Kelly) schedule. I don't know if they still do it to this day. The problem with the 4/10 is covering open shifts. Filling the first or last couple of hours is easy, but who works the middle part of the shift? How long can you order an employee to work in one 24 hour day without some time off between shifts to sleep (allowing for drive-time between work and home)? Supervisors must consider the alertness level of dispatch personnel verses the 'warm-body' syndrome of filling a seat at a console.

What is the population of the jurisdiction of your agency?

Less than 5,000 **7%**
5,000 to 10,000 **12%**
10,000 to 50,000 **32%**
50,000 to 100,000 **12%**
100,000 to 500,000 **17%**
500,000+ **12%**

The obvious conclusion here is activity generated by more people. Small, local areas have the advantage that dispatch personnel know the community and its concerns. As the numbers go up, so do the problems (gang, drugs, more medicals or fires, and other types of crime). The other aspect of a larger population group is the area covered. Can the Telecommunicators know the jurisdiction as well in a large area (say the entire State) as well as dispatchers in a smaller area?

Thank you to everyone who participated by filling out the forms, and to those who added the extra comments at the end: bless you. I know you are all busy and I do appreciate the time it took to answer the questions!

Helpful Websites

This list is a tiny sampling of the resources out there. Most of these sites listed have additional links provided, some generic Public Safety and others specific to dispatching.

911 Cares website
www.911cares.com

911 Lifeline website
www.911lifeline.org

911 Magazine online
www.911magazine.com

911 Resource Center
www.911.gov

Associated Public Safety Communications Officials, Inc, International (APCO)
www.apcointl.org

Copshock – stress issues
www.copshock.com

EMS1 emergency medical services news
www.ems1.com

Federal Communications Commission
www.fcc.gov

Firehouse Magazine
www.firehousemagazine.com

FIRESCOPE
www.firescope.org

What is Your Emergency? The History of Public Safety Dispatching in America

Headset911 – a blog on dispatchers and stress
www.headsets911.blogspot.com

Incident Dispatch Resource Center
www.incidentdispatch.net

International Academies of Emergency Dispatch
www.emergencydispatch.org

Journal of Emergency Medical services (JEMS)
www.jems.com

National Center for Missing and Exploited Children
www.missingkids.com

Federal Emergency Management Authority (FEMA)
www.fema.gov

National Emergency Communications Institute
www.nec911.com

National Emergency Number Association (NENA)
www.nena.org

National Telecommunications and Information Administration (NTIA)
www.ntia.doc.gov

PoliceOne news and information on law enforcement
www.policeone.com

Telecommunicator Emergency Response Taskforce (TERT)
http://njti-tert.org

Bibliography

Associated Public Safety Communications Officials International, Inc website
9-1-1 Resources, APCO Projects
www.apcointl.org

APCO Professional Communications Human Resources Taskforce
Challenges Facing 9-1-1 Public Safety Communications Professionals, 2nd Edition
August 2011, APCO

Auf der Heide, Erik, M.D.
Disaster Response: Principles of Preparation and Coordination
1989, The C.V. Mosby Company, St. Louis, MO

Battles, Kathleen
Calling All Cars: Radio Dragnets and the Technology of Policing
2010, University of Minnesota Press, Minneapolis
Kindle edition

Behr, Richard
Under the Headset: Surviving Dispatcher Stress
2000 Staggs Publishing, Wildomar, CA

Boyd, Jeryy, M.S. and Dave Larton
Incident Dispatcher: A Guide for the Professional Tactical and Incident Dispatcher
2007, First Contact 9-1-1, LLC Publisher, Morgan Hill, CA

Burke, Rick and Joe Ross
Side by Side, Step by Step
Urgent Communications Magazine, April 2013

Burks, John and George Hall

What is Your Emergency? The History of Public Safety Dispatching in America

Working Fire: The San Francisco Fire Department
1982 Chronicle Books, San Francisco, CA, 1985 edition

Burton, Alan
Police Telecommunications
1973 Charles C. Thomas Publishers, Springfield, Illinois

Burton, Alan
Article on 911 history
Dispatch Monthly website

Callahan, James A., Fire Chief, St. Petersburg, Florida
Civil Disturbances
USFA Technical Series Report #98
1996 October-November

Clawson, Jeff J, M.D. and Kate Boyd Democoeur, EMT-P
Principles of Emergency Medical Dispatch
1988 Prentice Hall, New Jersey

Committee of Trauma and the Committee on Shock
Accidental Death and Disability: the Neglected Disease of Modern Society
1996 Division of Medical Services, National Academy of Sciences, National Research Council, Washington, D.C.

Cooper, Martin
The Many Faces of Radio
Radio Club of America DVD

Daily Chronicle article
City Lightning: How the Fire Alarm Telegraph is Worked
February 11, 1897
San Francisco Fire Dept museum website

Dispatch Monthly website

by Diana Sprain

www.dispatchmonthly.com

East Bay Hills Fire Operations Review Group
The East Bay Hills Fire: Report to Elihu Harris, Mayor of Oakland, and Loni Hancock, Mayor of Berkeley
27th February, 1992, State of California, Governor's Office of Emergency Services

www.emergencydispatch.org
The development of Emergency Medical Dispatch in the USA: a historical perspective
National Academy of Emergency Dispatch articles

Federal Communications Commission
E9-1-1/TTY Compatibility Status Report
November 11, 1999, CC Docket No. 94-102
www.fcc.gov

Federal Communications Commission
Legal and Regulatory Framework for Next Generation 911 Services Report to Congress and Recommendations
Feb 22, 2013, Pursuant to the Next Generation 911 Advancement Act of 2012
(Pub. L. No. 112-96 (2012))

Federal Communications Commission
Public Safety and Homeland Security Bureau Seeks to Refresh the Record Regarding Options for Addressing Non Emergency Calls to 911 From Non-Service Initiated Handsets
PS Docket No. 08-51, March 14, 2002

FEMA, U.S. Fire Administration
A Needs Assessment of the U.S. Fire Service,
December 2002 Publication FA-240

Firescope: highlights of the evolution of Incident Command System as developed by

FIRESCOPE
www.firescope.org

Fire Task Force
Report of Task Force to Recommend Action to Reduce the
Chances of Men Being Killed
Burning While Fighting Fire
1957, Forest Service, United State Department of Agriculture

Foster, Raymond E. (Lt. LAPD – Ret.)
A Concise History of American Policing
Kindle edition

Haleyville Fire Department website
www.haleyvillefire.org

Holland, Michael Sgt (Ret.)
Berkeley Police Dept. Ca
Personal Correspondence
February 2013

Homeland Security
Wanton Violence at Columbine High School
USFA-TR-128, April 1999

Jackson, Penny
"A Stormy Response"
Urgent Communications Magazine
September 2012

Jager, Eric
The Last Duel
2004, Broadway Books, New York, NY

Kates, Allen R.
CopShock: Surviving Posttraumatic Stress Disorder (PTSD)
1999, Holbrook Street Press, Tucson, AZ, 2010 edition

Kenlon, John
Fires and Firefighters
1913, Grace H. Doran Company, New York

Larson, Randall
Personal Correspondence
January 2013

Larson, Randall
Ten Years of 9-1-1 Magazine – A history in 4000 Words or So
Jan/Feb 1999, Mar/Apr 1999, and May/Jun 1999 issues of 911 Magazine
9-1-1 Magazine

Larson, Randall
The Shooting at Virginia Tech
Jan/Feb 2008 issue of 9-1-1 Magazine

Lawrence, Edward, reporter
Las Vegas 8 News Now, Eyewitness News
October 8, 2007
"New Details About a Runaway Rail Car Carrying Chlorine"

Leonard, V.A.
The Police Communications System
1970 Charles C. Thomas Publishers, Springfield, Illinois

Lyndon B. Johnson Library Archieves (via Dispatch Monthly website)
Challenge of Crime In a Free Society A Report to the President's Commission on Law Enforcement and Adminsstration of Justice
The Institute for Defense Analysis

Lyndon B. Johnson Library Archieves (via Dispatch Monthly website)

What is Your Emergency? The History of Public Safety Dispatching in America

Comments of The Federal Communications Commission On
H. Con. Res. 361, 90th
Congress, 1st Session, A House Concurrent Resolution That Would Express The Sense Of
Congress That The United States Should Have One Uniform Nationwide Fire Reporting Telephone Number And One Uniform Nationwide Police Reporting Telephone Number.

Management Analysis, Inc.
Management Efficiency Assessment of the Interagency Wildland Fire Dispatch and Related
Services
2008 US Forest Service / Dept. of the Interior Report

Mazerole, Lorraine and Dennis Rogan (and others)
Managing Calls to the Police with 911/311 Systems
October 2001, National Institute of Justice, Research for Practice,
United States Department of Justice, Washington, D.C.
Kindle edition

Metropolitan Area Communications Center Overview
April 2012, Centennial, CO

Moore, Linda K.
Emergency Communications: Broadband and the Future of 911
Kindle version

National Archives website
www.archives.gov

National Commission on Fire Prevention and Control
America Burning: The Report of the National Commission on Fire Prevention and Control
4th May, 1973, U.S. Government, Washington, D.C.

website
http://www.emergencydispatch.org/

National Emergency Number Association (NENA) and the Association of Public-Safety Communications Officials (APCO)
2012 Public Safety Considerations for Smartphone App developers

National Emergency Number Association website
www.nena.org

National Fire Protection Agency
www.NFPA.org
The Third Needs Assessment of the U.S. Service
NFPA Fire Analysis & Research
June 2011, Quincy MA

Nichols-Pethick, Jonathan
TV Cops – The Contemporary American Television Police Drama
2012 Routledge, New York NY

Page, James O.
The Paramedics
1979, Backdraft Publications, Morristown, NJ

Parker, Alfred E.
Crime Fighter: August Vollmer
1961 the MacMillan Company, New York

Peck, Mark
Personal Correspondence
January 2013
Director, Virtual EMS Museum

Pivetta, Sue

What is Your Emergency? The History of Public Safety Dispatching in America

91-1: An Emerging 'Hidden' Career
9-1-1 Magazine On-line

Pivetta, Sue
The Exceptional Trainer: A No-Nonsense Guide for the Trainers of Emergency Communications
2005, Professional Pride Publishing, Sumner, WA 2nd edition

Post, Carl J.
Omaha Orange: A Popular History of EMS in America
2002, Jones and Bartlett Publishers, Sudbury, MA, 2nd edition

Praschak, Mark
"Medic 16, Medic 16": The Chronicles of a Street Medic
Kindle version

Public Safety Communications
The Lifeline of Public Safety; the Status of the Profession, Challenges, Faced, and the for Need Change 2nd edition
August 2011 APCO Professional Communications Human Resources Taskforce
APCO International, Inc.

Radio Club of America website
www.radioclubofamerica.org
biography of Frank A. Gunther, 1908-1999

Radio Club of America
76th Anniversary Diamond Jubilee Yearbook
1984 Radio Club of America

Rath, David
"The NG911 Funding Gap"
Emergency Management Magazine
Summer 2016

Reppetto, Thomas A.
American Police: The Blue Parade 1845-1945 A History
1978, Enigma Books
Kindle edition

Rigg, Nancy J.
Shoot-Out In North Hollywood: Command and Communications
Sept/Oct 1997 issue 9-1-1 Magazine

Rossamundo, Christina
Wildlands Fire Management-Federal Policies and Their Implications for Local Departments
United States Fire Administration, Publication TR-045

Rothman, Hal K.
Blazing Heritage – A History of Wildland Fire in the National Parks
2007, Oxford University Press, New York

Routley, J. Gordon
Massive Leak of Liquefied Chlorine Gas, Henderson, NV
May 1991, U.S. Fire Administration/Technical Report Series number 052

Rybicki, Rich APCO Historical Committee Chair and Keri Losavio Public Safety
Communications Editor
The Evolution of Public Safety Radio
April 2010, Public Safety Communications Magazine

www.Sfmuseum.org
City lightning: How the Fire Alarm Telegraph is Worked

Shapiro, Arnold
Personal interview via telephone
September 16, 2013

What is Your Emergency? The History of Public Safety Dispatching in America

Smith, Paul
Executive Director, MetComm
Email correspondence, June 2013

Spahn, Edwin J.
Fire Service Radio Communications
1989 Fire Engineering, New York NY

Standard for Telecommunicator Emergency Response Taskforce (TERT) Deployment
By the National Joint TERT Initiative (NJTI) & NENA Contingency Planning Committee
27, May, 2009, APCO Publication APCO/NENA ANS1.105.1-2009

Steele, Susi B
Emergency Dispatching: A Medical Communicators Guide
1993 Regents/Prentice Hall, Upper Saddle River, NJ

Stewart, James K.
Independent Board of Inquiry Into the Oakland Police Department: March 21, 2009
Incident A Public Report of Findings and Recommendations
Prepared by the Independent Board of Inquiry
December 2009, Institute For Public Research

Stratus Technologies
How Does Your PSAP Stack Up?
October 2012 Public Safety Survey Results, Stratus Technologies
www.stratus.com

Theil, Adam K.
Special Report: Improving Firefighter Communications
January 1999, U.S. Fire Administration/Technical Report Series #99

Theil, Adam K.
The Aftermath of Firefighter Fatality Incidents: Preparing for the Worst (Special Report)
10, October 1984, FEMA Special Report #89

Varone, Curt
Firefighter Safety and Radio Communication
3-01-03 FE Network Online
Fire Life FE University Urban Firefighter Fire Apparatus Magazine

Walsh, Brian Evard, PhD Mnlp JP (ret)
Emergency Responder Communications Skills Handbook
2010, Walsh Seminars Ltd., Victoria, British Columbia

Wildfire Lessons Learned Center
Initial Impressions: Southern California Fires 2007, What We Learned, How We Worked
Report by the Wildfire Lessons Learned Center
Tucson, AZ

Yokley, Richard and Rozane Sutherland
Emergency! Behind the Scene
2008 Jones and Bartlett Publishers, Sudbury, Massachusetts

What is Your Emergency? The History of Public Safety Dispatching in America

Author Biography

Diana Sprain works as a Public Safety Dispatcher for the law enforcement division of the Nevada Department of Wildlife. She is a POST-certified Dispatcher, Tactical Dispatcher, Civilian Training Officer, and Supervisor with over 25 years experience. In addition, she is a licensed and certified Pharmacy Technician. Prior to becoming a Public Safety Dispatcher, she worked as an Emergency Medical Technician in Los Angeles County (CA) and Oakland (CA). She is the author of the fictional fantasy series *Greycliff Chronicles*.

Diana is a member of the Associated Public Safety Communications Officials (APCO), the National Emergency Number Association (NENA), the Public Safety Writer's Association, and the Sierra Writers Group. You can read about her novels and her posts on her blog:

www.dianasprain.net

CPSIA information can be obtained
at www.ICGtesting.com
Printed in the USA
LVHW022056140721
692685LV00010B/649